AF255655

God Speaks His Love

God Speaks His Love

—— Daniel Lloyd ——

WIPF & STOCK · Eugene, Oregon

GOD SPEAKS HIS LOVE

Wipf & Stock
An Imprint of Wipf and Stock Publishers
199 W. 8th Ave., Suite 3
Eugene, OR 97401

www.wipfandstock.com

PAPERBACK ISBN: 978-1-6667-3668-7
HARDCOVER ISBN: 978-1-6667-9540-0
EBOOK ISBN: 978-1-6667-9541-7

01/03/23

This book is dedicated to Amy, who couldn't be
more loving and supportive.

Contents

Preface

Why another book on the Scriptures? That is a serious question to ask, since there already exists a mountain of books and study programs.

Let me begin by making a few general comments. First, it is the joyful duty of Christians to learn about and study the Scriptures. I say "duty" in the same way we would say that it is the duty of a parent to continue to speak to, and learn about, his children. Building relationships is a joy, and the study of Scripture is a God-prescribed way of building a better relationship with the Father, Son, and Holy Spirit. This is a life-long process, and it makes life sweeter, better, and more fulfilling.

Second, we occupy a particular time and place in history. It is good in some ways to hear from contemporary members of the church. This certainly does not mean that other generations do not have tremendous value for us. For example, watching and reading Bishop Fulton Sheen's work continues to be a source of inspiration and knowledge which enables us to encounter God and the church more deeply. But most people still want to see contemporaries speak of old things in new ways. The experience for the speaker/writer, the listener/reader, and the ensuing sense of dialogue gives all involved a unique experience of the vitality of God's presence in the church. God's presence remains just as clear and as strong as it was in generations past.

Third, the life-long process of encountering the Scriptures should be understood as similar to a relationship whose dimensions can never be exhausted or fully known. We know our spouses, our children, our parents, and our friends intimately. But we also know that our short lives on this earth will never equate to knowing them fully. For this reason, we find even our oldest and best understood relationships always new and refreshing because of the energy, support, comfort, challenge, and richness we receive through each other as we progress forward in our relationships.

Why then this book? As a selected journey through some carefully chosen scriptural texts, this book seeks to nourish those who want to learn more about God, listen to God, and see new dimensions in the relationships we have with God and each other. Some studies introduce readers to all the books in the Bible. Some cover one or a few. Some books focus on a theme or several themes. All such studies are of great value over the course of lifetime study because they provide different ways of engaging the Scriptures—of listening to and talking with God. This book is designed in the manner of the last group mentioned above, that of a focus on a theme. Of course, reading the Scriptures themselves must be the ultimate focus, but having a companion along the way is almost always helpful.

The major theme found in this book is God's love. Tied to investigating this theme will be a whole host of related topics, such as God's historical activities which culminate in coming to earth himself as Jesus. But that is just the beginning of the story. The story picks up steam when people hear about the events surrounding God's work and then allow God to start reshaping their entire lives. This book is very much about the transformation in which all human beings are called to participate. It is a transformation based on God's healing love, which in turn allows people to shape all of their relationships on the basis of the kind of love which is understandable through the Scriptures.

This book can be used as an introduction for those without much knowledge of, or experience reading, the Bible. Therefore, this book can serve as an important exposure to Bible study and to ideas central to Christianity. It can also be used by those who simply want to see some familiar texts united through the lens of love.

Primarily though, it can be used as a tool for anyone interested in getting a taste for the life-long practice of encountering God through the Scriptures. It is written to be engaging for individuals, small groups, and as a supplement to undergraduate courses.

Acknowledgements

Many thanks to Dr. Michael Anthony Novak and Dr. Thomas Humphries for their careful reading of the book and for their many helpful suggestions and corrections. Thanks also to Anna Lloyd, who read much of this work and helped me improve it. I would also like to thank Dcn. Brian Justice for his insightful suggestions and comments on the beginning chapters. Of course, any error in the final product is my own. Thank you to Amy, Anna, Owen, and Miles, who always encourage me. I am eternally grateful to have such generous friends and family members.

Introduction

In His goodness and wisdom God chose to reveal Himself and to make known to us the hidden purpose of His
will (cf. Eph. 1:9) by which through Christ, the Word
made flesh, man might in the Holy Spirit have access
to the Father and come to share in the divine nature
(cf. Eph. 2:18; 2 Pet. 1:4). Through this revelation, therefore, the invisible God (cf. Col. 1:15, 1 Tim. 1:17) out
of the abundance of His love speaks to men as friends
(cf. Exod. 33:11; John 15:14–15) and lives among them
(cf. Bar. 3:38), so that He may invite and take them into
fellowship with Himself.[1]

God has never been, nor will ever be, silent. Christianity
knows a God who communicates. Central to this communication is the Christian affirmation that God is love by nature and
acts out of his love. God created us out of love and always seeks
to give us healing and life. These assertions are some of the most
basic principles of the Christian faith. The passage above, taken
from the document *Dei Verbum* (Latin for *The Word of God*), was
written by the bishops of the Catholic Church during the Second
Vatican Council (Vatican II), which took place from 1962–1965. It
succinctly makes some of these basic points. This book will follow
the path set out with these ideas.

---

1. Vatican II. *Dogmatic Constitution on Divine Revelation/Dei Verbum*. sec.
2. https://www.vatican.va/archive/hist_councils/ii_vatican_council/documents/
vat-ii_const_19651118_dei-verbum_en.html.

There are many ways to write books about particular topics. This book begins by acknowledging Jesus (God come to earth united to a human nature) as the fullness of God's revelation and as the culmination of God's communication as especially found in the Scriptures. A different way to have written the book might have been to present selected biblical texts chronologically. The passages could be mined for related themes and ideas from the perspective of historical development. Then the concluding chapters could be used to address Jesus **Christ** as the surprising fullness of revelation which both conforms to and expands upon the Scriptures already seen.[2] But the structure of this book is intended to begin with as much clarity about the Christian understanding of God and his communication with us as possible.

The Trinity: The One God Is the Father, Son, and Holy Spirit

The Christian understanding of God needs to be described before we begin wrestling with the Scriptures. When many people say "God," what they mean is the "Father." Furthermore, when some people read the passage in the prior paragraph about Jesus as the fullness of God's revelation, they read it with same understanding. They read it with the thinking that God and Jesus are different. This is not what Christianity teaches because it basically translates to saying that God is one Person and Jesus is a different person. The trouble with this thinking is that it would also mean that Jesus himself is not God, and that is the opposite of what Christianity teaches. The idea that God is one, singular Person only is the foundation of Jewish and Islamic faith. However, this is not the case with Christianity, because Christians believe that God revealed himself to be a Trinity of Persons. This leads Christians to use the word "God" to speak about the one God who is the Father, the Son, and the Holy Spirit. The doctrine of the **Trinity** can then be briefly described as: the reality that the One God, or the one

2. Bolded words in the text indicates that the term appears in the glossary at the end of this book.

divine nature, can only be understood as the distinct Persons of the Father, Son, and Holy Spirit, who, because they share the one divine nature, are each fully God. This is the reason why it is customary for Christians to pray sometimes to the distinct Persons. At other times, Christians praying to "God" are often praying to the Trinity of Persons, though they might at other times identify one of the three Persons simply as "God."

An example might help to illustrate the ideas presented above about the Trinity. In the catechism (a book of Christian teachings) which I have used with my own children, there is a little comic strip with four panes. The first pane has a man asking a child: "What are you?" The boy responds: "I am a boy." The second pane has the man asking: "Who are you?" The boy responds: "Eddie Smith." Then, the third pane switches to the boy speaking to God. It has the boy asking God: "What are you?" God responds: "God." The boy then asks in the fourth pane: "Who are you?" God responds: "The Father, Son, and Holy Spirit . . . (God)."[3] This is a helpful way of teaching children that Christianity often uses the word "God" to refer to the union of the three Persons of the Father, Son, and Holy Spirit.

Christians also use the word "God" personally in conversations and prayers. It is traditional to refer to God with masculine pronouns (he/him/his). Though these are singular pronouns, Christians still use these terms with the belief in the Trinity in the background. This pronoun use, therefore, can be quite confusing. If God is Tri-Personal (i.e. really the Father, Son, and Holy Spirit), then why do Christians use singular pronouns? Christians refer to the one God with he/him/his because God is both the one, supreme being, and because God is first and foremost personal (Tri-personal in fact!). Although it can be traditional to talk about the Father specifically as God and to believe that any Christian reference to God with the words "he," "him," and "his" is a reference to the Father, this is not always the case. It might sometimes be the case, but any teaching which tries to technically make the Father

3. Saint Joseph Baltimore Catechism, rev. ed. (New York: Catholic Book Publishing, 1969), 22.

alone always synonymous with the words "God," "he," "him," or "his" has always been rejected by Christianity. Again, technically, if Christians are calling the Christian God "he," it is because of the radically transcendent personhood of the Father, Son, and Holy Spirit in their unity as the one God.

The major consequence of belief in the Trinity is the knowledge that God is by nature perfectly loving (1 John 4:16). The Father loves the Son and Holy Spirit; the Son loves the Father and the Holy Spirit; the Holy Spirit loves the Father and Son. We can even say that, in a sense, the nature of the one God is love. God by nature loves and communicates love, because the one God is the Father, Son, and Holy Spirit. This has significant consequences for a book such as this on God's loving communication as found in the Scriptures.

Taking the doctrine of the Trinity seriously also means ridding ourselves of the idea that God begins communicating at a time and place. Such thinking would only make sense if the one God is only one Person. If God is a singular Person, then God could really only be thought of as communicating and loving *after* he made someone to love and with whom to communicate. Christianity does not think of God this way. Christianity's doctrine of the Trinity affirms that the Father, Son, and Holy Spirit communicate perfect love eternally. "Eternally" means outside of creation with its structure of time and space. This also means that God's creation of, and communication with, human beings is the gift of a participation in God's loving life. To bring these ideas together, we can say, first, that God is eternally communicating love since God is eternally Father, Son, and Holy Spirit. Second, we can say that creation exists because the Father, Son, and Holy Spirit chose to share this divine life of love in a special way with human beings. We human beings were created for the primary purpose of being able to share in loving relationships with God and each other.

Lastly, we will see that some of the biblical language about God seems to defy trinitarian beliefs, which is described above as the fundamental Christian belief. Biblical authors, for example, often do use the word "God" as synonymous with "the Father." Examples include:

- "For God so loved the world that he gave his only Son, so that everyone who believes in him might not perish but might have eternal life" (John 3:16).

- " . . . yet for us there is one God, the Father, from whom all things are and for whom we exist, and one Lord, Jesus Christ, through whom all things are and through whom we exist" (1 Cor 8:6).

- "Therefore, he (Jesus) is always able to save those who approach God through him, since he lives forever to make intercession for them" (Heb 7:25).

At least three things are happening in these examples. First, these biblical authors represent some of the first expressions of Christian faith, and these expressions are not yet developed in a consistently technical way. Reading these texts apart from the faith of the church and apart from the clearer developments in the expression of the church misses the deeper and clearer understanding of these texts which actually support trinitarian belief. Second, other elements in the biblical texts conflict with understanding these texts at just their face value. Many other passages, for example, point especially to Jesus' divinity and equality with the Father. Third, over time the church came to clearer expressions about the nature of God as Father, Son, and Holy Spirit. These expressions became the framework by which to read the above texts. Because of these interconnected elements, the Christian community correctly reads the above texts as plainly giving witness to the Trinity, even if those outside the Christian faith community might misunderstand them.

General Revelation and Special Revelation

Now that we have the Christian view of encounter with the God who is Father, Son, and Holy Spirit, we can make a few comments about the nature of God's communication with creation. Traditionally, Christianity speaks about two kinds of communication. They are sometimes called "general revelation" and "special revelation." Before describing them, it is important to note that Christianity does not really make a hard and fast line between these, at least in terms of God's intentionality. God (as Father, Son, and Holy Spirit) is lovingly communicative by nature. When God creates, it is for the purpose of sharing this eternally loving communication and communing with us. The word "revelation" used above about God's communication comes from the Latin word meaning "to uncover or show." To speak then of kinds of revelation, we are simply acknowledging that God communicates with us in more than one way. To put it another way, all forms of revelation will always be supportive of each other. They will never be opposed.

General revelation (which is synonymous with the term "natural revelation") starts with the fact that God made human beings as rational beings with free will. These attributes give us the ability to know things about God both from our own nature as human beings and through the world which God made for us. This form of revelation can be thought of as a kind of built-in communication from God. We can, for example, investigate our understanding of ourselves as human beings. For almost all human beings in history, this has meant recognizing that we have both a spiritual and a physical nature. We are souls and bodies. Having a spiritual nature has led almost all human beings to recognize, therefore, that we are more than just our bodies and that some kind of creator gave us these complicated natures. These beliefs about being physical and spiritual have led many to believe in some kind of creative spiritual higher power with which we have some natural similarity, especially in our spiritual dimension. These ideas fall within general revelation because we simply need to think about ourselves to say meaningful things about God.

We can mention a few other common reasons for believing in, and acknowledging, a creator God through general revelation. The first involves a reflection on the structure and order of the world. For much of human history, most people have looked at the order and structure of the world and saw good and clear reasons to believe in creation from a higher power. Although many bad things happen in this world, it is usually experienced as good and predictable. The second points to our ability to know right from wrong and good from evil. Many people think of morality as intuitive; we just know these things. To a certain extent, this is true. But most people believe that ideas such as love, justice, mercy, honesty, and self-sacrifice are not just pulled out of the air. To believe that there is a moral order in the world and that it is wrong to defy it seems to transcend cultures and human invention. Christianity points to both these sets of ideas, common to human life, and identifies them with natural revelation.

The other kind of revelation is called special revelation. Unlike general revelation, **special revelation** (synonymous with the term "historical revelation") involves God actively coming into contact with his creation in order to offer grace, love, and direction to human beings. Since Catholicism understands the Scriptures to have been written by people in communion with and inspired by God, the Bible is a good example of special revelation. Considering the event of God speaking to Moses while reading the book of Exodus is like considering a form of special revelation (God speaking specifically to Moses) within another form of special revelation (the inspired Scripture telling that story). The Bible recounts the ways in which God builds up his relationship with the Jews and the world. For Christians, the unquestionable climax of special revelation happened about 2,000 years ago when God the Son became the human being we know as Jesus. God himself took on our human nature in order to live with, teach, heal, nurture, and die for all of humanity. This joining of his divine nature to a human nature allows for his **resurrection** to bring healing to us and to bring us into fellowship with God. All of the ideas found in this paragraph, because they describe us as having a better understanding of God through his activities of reaching out to us, fit into the category of special revelation.

This book is an invitation to consider God's special revelations as witnessed to in the Bible. Among other events, it covers the events of God speaking to Moses out of the Burning Bush and then leading the Hebrews out of Egyptian slavery during the **Exodus**. It covers God giving messages to the Jewish prophets in order to help lead Israel. Significant time is spent with the New Testament authors telling us about the life and activities of God the Son when he took on a human nature and became known to us as Jesus. Finally, several chapters cover the elements of how the church began to live out its mission of being the community which God formed and continues to form.

God's special revelations as given in the Bible and lived in the church are nothing short of ways to experience true, abundant, and immortal life. God is recognized as Father, Son, and Holy Spirit. God is recognized as creating us and redeeming us from the sin and the death we have brought upon ourselves. Through his own death for us, God lovingly makes possible our embrace of the truths at the center of reality: God created us out of love, guides us out of love, redeems us out of love, and brings about everlasting life with him and each other for love.

Conclusion

The next chapter will address a few more specific ideas about how the church understands the Scriptures. This will include an emphasis on John's Gospel, the role of community in light of the Scriptures, the unity of both the Old and the New Testament, and the importance and nature of our response to God. Make sure to keep in mind these central ideas about both the Trinity and also the two forms of revelation. Whether stated or not, these ideas will be essential to our encounters with the biblical texts.

1

Encountering the Scriptures

Introduction

Have you ever seen a poster, a billboard, a shirt, or anything else with "John 3:16" on it? This is a popular biblical reference because it offers a succinct version of the message of Christianity. The verse itself says this: "For God so loved the world that he gave his only Son, so that everyone who believes in him might not perish but might have eternal life." There are many important ideas to be found in this text. Four of the most important are:

1. "God" refers to the one God of Israel. This is the one and only God with whom the Jewish people have been in relationship for nearly 4,000 years.

2. God loves us and does whatever is necessary to bring us healing and communion with him.

3. According to Christianity, "God" here refers to God the Father, and "Son" refers explicitly to Jesus. Jesus is God the Son (whom John also called the "Word") come as a human being.

4. Sharing in eternal life is somehow connected with believing God's Word and what God has done for us out of love, presumably through either seeing or hearing about the Word.

We can think of these ideas as central to the core of Christianity's understanding of faith. They are God's offer to us that he can transform our lives and actions. We will return frequently to these ideas throughout this book, but we should stop for a moment to appreciate how clearly the connection between God's love, God's desire for our healing, God's activity, and our response are given in this single verse. That appreciation is increased when we also realize that the Bible presents these same ideas in many of its chapters, books, and through a clear understanding of the Bible as a complete collection of books.

Before moving on, we can note several ways this current chapter is a little different than the rest of the book. First, this chapter is an introduction to a few foundational ideas which will guide the readings and activities of this book. We will use this chapter to explore a few important ideas about how the Scriptures are understood by the church. In chapter 2, we will get started on reading scriptural texts with short previews and then reflections on those texts.

Second, this chapter presents important ideas related to the way the Scriptures came about within the community of God's people. Some ideas from two very important documents will be used in this chapter to set up our journey through the Scriptures in the coming chapters. The first document is from the Second Vatican Council called *Dei Verbum* (*The Word of God*), written in 1965. This document lays out ideas about the Catholic Church's understanding of revelation and the Scriptures. The second text is called *Verbum Domini* (*The Word of the Lord*). It was written in 2010 by Pope Benedict XVI after a meeting of bishops. They were reflecting on the church's growth in understanding and applying the principles of *Dei Verbum* over the course of four and a half decades. Both of these texts are easily found on the internet and on the Vatican website.[1] Also, both texts are important and quite enjoyable reading for any Catholic interested in how the church thinks of Scripture and revelation.

---

1. *Dei Verbum* can be found at the following web address: https://www. vatican.va/archive/hist_councils/ii_vatican_council/documents/vat-ii_ const_19651118_dei-verbum_en.html. *Verbum Domini* can be found at the following web address: https://www.vatican.va/content/benedict-xvi/en/apost _exhortations/documents/hf_ben-xvi_exh_20100930_verbum-domini.html.

Importance of John's Gospel

This chapter began with a quotation from John's Gospel, specifically John 3:16. What makes this Gospel so important from the time of the early church all the way up to today is that it shows the continuity of God's words and actions throughout all of time. John is careful to connect creation, as found in Genesis (the very first book of the Scriptures), to the coming of God as the human being Jesus. Here again, we see special emphasis on the fact that God's words and actions must be seen in the combined witnesses of the Old Testament books (written before the **Incarnation**) and the New Testament books (written after the Incarnation). Together, these books of the Old and New Testaments are what Christians call the Bible.

John begins his Gospel by using the Greek word *logos*, which we translate as "Word," and he presents this "Word" as being with God (the Father) and also being God himself. John then identifies the Word as the Son, and a bit later he also identifies this Word/Son as Jesus. Before looking at the first verse in John, notice that John's Gospel clearly asserts the Person who is the Word/Son/Jesus is God like the Father is God. John 1:1 states, "In the beginning was the Word, and the Word was with God, and the Word was God." Keeping in mind that the early Christian authors were needing to create new language to express the Christian mystery as outlined in the Introduction of this book, we can see that the meaning in John 1:1 of "the Word was with God" is the following: the Son (who is called the Word here) was with the Father (who is simply called "God" here).

But how can Christians make the assertion that the Son (along with the Father and Spirit, of course) are together before all time? Christianity uses the word "eternal" for this idea. We look especially to John 1:1's use of the word "beginning." Anyone at all familiar with the opening of Genesis cannot miss the connection John is making with the idea that God (the Father) uses his Word (the Son) for creation. Genesis 1:1–3 states: "In the beginning, when God created the heavens and the earth—and the earth was without form or shape, with darkness over the abyss and the mighty wind (or "Spirit") sweeping over the waters—Then God said: Let there be light, and there was light." We will see more of John's use of Genesis in chapter 5, but pointing out this connection between Genesis's account of creation and John's emphasis that it was the Word who helped create is the important thing to keep in mind. All of the above means that Christians cannot read the first verses of Genesis without seeing the Father, Son, and Holy Spirit at work, and Christians cannot read any part of the Bible without seeing a complete continuity in the way God revealed himself more and more fully to humanity.

The Unity of the Testaments

As should be clear now, Christian references to the Word are always essentially personal, since the "Word" is another name for the Son. Christianity, however, also recognizes that the Scriptures point to the story of God's **special revelations**, which are God's direct activities in the world. These texts of the Bible are also properly referred to as "God's Word." Such uses of "Word," for both the Son and for the Scriptures, are not competitive. God the Son is the Word, and humanity knows the most about God and God's activities through his communication to us as Jesus. But, God also communicates in a special way through the set of texts identified as the Bible. This set of books is a special gift written by the faith community under the guidance of the Holy Spirit.

The Bible, as we have it, was written over the course of many centuries and by many different authors. Over this time, the community of faith developed in its relationship with God as well as in the information God revealed about himself through his action. The ultimate form of special revelation was God the Son who came as Jesus. The theological term for this event is called the Incarnation. "**Incarnation**" means: God's coming in the flesh. For these reasons, Christians understand the Bible as giving increasing clarity about God's activities and revelations to the faith community. This is sometimes called progressive revelation. Just like in any normal relationship, people reveal more and more about themselves over time. One example of this is seen in the passage of Genesis quoted above. The author of Genesis and all subsequent generations of the Jewish people have believed that the one God created all things and created all things good. For those living before the coming of Jesus, there really was no way for the author of Genesis or its readers to understand Genesis's creation account in terms of the activity of the Father, Son, and Holy Spirit. John's Gospel made the point that the God who is **Trinity** (Father, Son, and Holy Spirit) created together. Many other parts of the Old Testament were made clearer by Jesus' coming through this same idea of progressive revelation.

We have already seen that **general revelation** is connected to the ability of all human beings to come to certain knowledge about God, human beings, and creation in general, just by virtue of having been created by God as rational creatures. Elements of general revelation are found throughout the Old and New Testaments, but the Bible overall is mostly about God's special revelations, which shape communities of his own creation. Apart from the very early instances of God interacting with human beings in general, the Old Testament is about God forming and interacting with the Jewish community in a special way. As we will see in the next chapter, the Jewish people come from Abraham and Sarah. This family, this tribe, wrote many inspired books based upon their experience of their special relationship with God. These texts which are inspired by the Holy Spirit are called the Old Testament, and they are mostly about the very special relationship God formed with the Jews.

It is the New Testament, however, which is the set of books about God the Son coming as Jesus to his people, the Jews. The New Testament is understood by Christianity to be the fulfillment, or next step, in the story begun in the Old Testament. These books teach about God bringing his plan to fulfillment by opening up the special relationship (a **covenant**) he made with the Jews to all human beings everywhere. Because of this, Christianity sees itself through the lens of the various Old Testament prophecies which predicted the unity of humankind under the God of Israel's reign.

This story about all human beings begins in the Old Testament with the creation of the world, progresses to the special relationship with the Jews through Abraham and Sarah, and continues through the tumultuous life of Israel as a nation. This same story climaxes in God coming himself as Jesus to teach us, minister to us, die for us, and be resurrected in both his body and soul for us. Although Christians believe that God came as Jesus to open the doors of his special relationship with the Jews to all people, Christians continue to believe that the Old Testament is a necessary and God-inspired part of the Bible. Because the story of God's relationship with all people unfolds over time, Christians believe that the Old Testament finds its deepest meaning with the revelation of the Incarnation and the life of Christian faith in the church.

The Word in the Community

Much was said in the prior section about the community of God's people. In Christianity, the phrase "community of God's people" means explicitly the church. The church is the community established by God for all human beings to be united in worship of, and service to, the one God. This church grew out of, and has its roots still within, the Jewish people as a special family which gave, and continues to give, witness to the one God. The emphasis on community is always a central feature of God's work. Love, after all, is only possible in a community. For this reason, we will see that God (who is the community of the Father, Son, and the Holy Spirit) made us in his image and likeness specifically to share in relationships. We will also see that God reveals himself to both individuals and to communities for the benefit of building and strengthening communities. As noted, when God called Abraham, he did so in order to gather a people, the Jewish people, into a special relationship with him.

Three important points, though often missed, concern the nature of the Bible in relation to the community. The first point many people miss is that the communities which God creates (first Israel and then the church) existed before the Scriptures were written. The

Scriptures were not written first and then became the thing around which a community of faith formed. Secondly, the Scriptures were composed by people already living within the community of faith, working under the guidance of the Spirit, and doing so in order to produce texts for the community of faith. Finally, the third point which many people miss is that these texts were not created by individuals for individuals only. These books of the Bible were only recognized as sacred because the community of faith could see the Spirit's work in them and in their benefit to the community. These three ideas are the reason why it is the community of faith which ultimately determines what these texts mean. The biblical books were written within the community, for the community, and must be interpreted by the community.

The above points might seem confusing. After all, many people have not thought much about where the Scriptures came from or how it is they came to have the status of being believed as uniquely inspired texts. One thing to consider is the fact that any written text, just like a movie or a song, might be interpreted in a variety of ways. The sacred Scriptures are no different. For example, Christians for nearly 2,000 years have argued about important interpretations of certain key texts. How are these arguments settled when different interpretations cannot exist together? What is to be done when, for instance, one interpreter says that the Gospels teach that Jesus is not really God and another interpreter says that the Gospels do indeed teach that Jesus is God. These two interpretations cannot coexist. When it comes to such conflicts, it is always the church community which can see the right interpretation.

When we realize then that the church possessed, lived, and preached the faith *before* the existence of the New Testament, then we can start to appreciate that the Scriptures themselves are the creation of the church community. Moreover, we can also say that every aspect of faith was not written about, or intended to be written about, in the books of the Bible. In general, the existence of the church's teachings and practices are called Tradition. Tradition is both tied to, but also more expansive than, the Scriptures. From the traditional historical perspective, Scripture and Tradition are both revelatory and guided by God. They coexist in harmony, since it is the same Holy Spirit who formed the church, guided the writing of the Scriptures, guides the church, and leads the church into properly interpreting the Scriptures.

Different Senses of the Scriptures

From the above section, it should be easy to predict that the Catholic Church teaches that the reading and interpretation of the Bible should be done from within the church. Since the Bible comes from the witness and life of the church, a correct understanding of the Scriptures will always be aligned to the beliefs and practices of the church. This statement may surprise some who are used to the idea that any text will have its most important meaning for an individual person through that individual's interpretation. The Bible does not work like this since the origin and nature of the Bible is not quite like any other text. Nevertheless, there are, of course, clear layers of the Scriptures which can be understood by everyone. In her interpretation, the church recognizes that there are various senses of the Scriptures, which can be seen even within a single verse.

The first sense to consider when reading Scripture is the literal, or historical, sense. The Bible often gives accounts of actual people in history as well as important historical events in which God plays a role. Christianity by nature has to be rooted in history, and it cannot be understood apart from history. Another way of putting it is that there is no such thing as Christian faith without its historical context. Christianity is not a philosophical system whose teachings can be divorced from history. As such, Christianity understands itself as only existing because God really did become the human being we know of as Jesus, who taught, healed, died, and was resurrected for our salvation. This statement allows us to make the following point about Christian interpretation of the Bible: there is usually a basic presumption about historical truth when the Scriptures are describing historical events, whether it is a description about Moses and the **Exodus**, the kingship of

David, the destruction of Israel and Judah by foreign invaders, the ministry of Jesus, or the growth of the early church.

Actions have meaning. Thus, there is always a second sense of Scripture, which is itself often divided into a few parts. This is the spiritual sense of Scripture. Christianity, like Judaism, has always acknowledged that the Scriptures are not just giving us an historical record. Rather, the spiritual senses of the Scriptures point to moral instruction, deeper teachings of the faith, as well as assurances about the life God is developing in us which will come to completion in heaven. Both senses of the Scriptures, the literal and the spiritual, are ultimately tied together in a way that all the senses find complementary meaning in and through each other.

We can look at John 3:16 to help us understand the application of the literal and spiritual methods of reading Scripture. Recall that 3:16 states: "For God so loved the world that he gave his only Son, so that everyone who believes in him might not perish but might have eternal life." The literal sense of this is a straightforward claim. About 2,000 years ago, the Father sent the Son to earth to become Jesus in order to bring about the possibility of salvation. The various spiritual senses are also apparent. What people believe about the Son includes all of his teachings while he ministered on earth. Many of the Son's teachings give us the moral standards God expects from us. Therefore, the moral sense of Scripture is embedded in this text. Additionally, John 3:16 presumes teachings directly related to the faith of Christianity. This text depends on John 1:1 and, therefore, can only be understood in light of the belief that the Son is God just as the Father is God. Implied in this statement is the reality that only God's sacrifice (i.e. Jesus' death and **resurrection**) can bring life. Finally, the reference to "eternal life" is a clear indication of the ultimate, heavenly goal of human existence. God's desire for us is that we be healed, saved, and perfected as human beings so as to share everlasting life with God and each other.

Conclusion

Many people today (sometimes even Christians!) misunderstand the Bible when they think of it as just ancient writings, written by ancient authors, which speak to ancient peoples about ancient problems. It is relatively common to hear such ideas in the mainstream media, entertainment, or on social media. Sometimes the statement goes something like: we are more advanced as people and as a society, and therefore these old writings have nothing to offer modern society. But this is the opposite of how Christians read the Bible.

Reading the Bible with a heart open to God reveals that all human beings, no matter where or when we live, struggle with the same kinds of issues in life. All human beings suffer through the sins of their cultures and families. Even more importantly, every human being suffers because of his own sins. Our personal sins cause ruptures in the relationships we have with God and with everyone in our lives. The Bible gives accounts of the deepest aspects of human experience and provides a life-giving witness to the healing God offers us.

Study and Reflection Questions

1. Do you think that many Christians have a hard time speaking about the ways the Father, Son, and Holy Spirit relate to each other? What is the best explanation which you have seen?

2. Have you ever heard or read someone claiming that the Old Testament and the New Testament do not really tell the same story about God? (You might have even heard the idea that the two Testaments are about different Gods!) What might the reasons be for such a position?

3. What is a benefit to the Catholic Church's understanding of the various senses of Scripture? What might be seen as a drawback to accepting various senses even of the same passage?

2

The Goodness of Creation
and the Fall to Violence

Preview

Genesis 1–11 includes stories related to the creation of the world, life in the Garden of Eden, the expulsion of Adam and Eve, an account of the first murder, the progression of sin and violence of all sorts, the story of Noah and the Flood, the repopulation of the nations, the story of the Tower of Babel, and finally some information about the family from which Abraham comes. There are enormous amounts of details in these stories which could be considered. In fact, the amount of spiritual and scholarly works dedicated to studying the smaller sections of these works in detail could fill a library. But this section of Genesis was also written to be read more quickly and with an eye towards seeing the main ideas connecting these parts as a narrative.

Before reading Gen 1–11, consider the fact that truth can be conveyed in more than one way and sometimes in several ways at once. Although the stories found in Gen 1–11 read like detailed history, many faithful Jews and Christians over the centuries have read these stories being less concerned with questions of archeology and being more concerned with how the details of the stories convey truth. In chapter 1, some attention was given to the senses of Scripture, namely the literal sense and the variety of spiritual senses. An example might be helpful here. The details related to the creation account, such as the six days of the creation and the day of rest, obviously direct the reader to ideas of God's organization and control over all things. But Christians and Jews have often explicitly rejected a focus on the literal reading of the text. Genesis 1 was not written to give a literal historical account during a specific week from a specific number of years ago, as if it was a news report. Rather, the details of the story, as will be discussed below, establish fundamental ideas that are true about God and God's relationship with creation. Once we know how the story goes, we must ask what it means.

Several central themes dominate Gen 1–11 and are key to understanding Gen 12–50. Genesis begins by presenting God's goodness and the goodness of all creation. This is the first major theme we will notice. Many people today who believe in God, but do not necessarily think of themselves as Christians, nevertheless also believe that God must be good and cannot do, or create, evil things. This has not always been the case. Many in the ancient world thought that the world included evil and that perhaps this evil came from the gods. In a revolutionary way which is often not appreciated today, Genesis's story of creation places goodness at the center of God's character and God's actions. This theme of goodness climaxes in the creation of human beings. God creates human beings in his image and likeness so that these creatures, Adam and Eve, can have relationships with him and also with each other.

A second theme concerns the entrance of sin into the world. Since God is perfectly good and only makes good things, Genesis presents sin and its consequences as coming from human free will. Those who ask why God would have created us with the tendency and capacity to sin and harm each other forget that having the initial choice to be good or evil is what defines us. It is our free will which allows us to have good relationships. It is also our free will which allows us to reject relationships and goodness in favor of selfishness and harmful desires. The story of Adam and Eve disobeying God in the Garden of Eden is the Bible's way of conveying the truths that God produces a good world, that the world in which we live is not what God intended, and that the responsibility for bringing evil in the world rests with our bad use of free will.

A third theme in these first 11 chapters of Genesis is the growth of sin in the lives of individuals and communities. Regardless of whether these stories were intended to be understood literally or as conveying truths through stories, most readers immediately recognize the reality of how sin works in the world. When we choose to sin, we often find ways to keep sinning in more and more ways. We also find many reasons to explain away our personal responsibility for sin. Such truths about the insidiousness and harm of sin are deeply embedded in these stories. These stories are also about providing a witness to the fact that God continues to respond to, and work with, the human children he created for good and holy relationships. We can think of this as a fourth and most important theme: God continues to respond to humanity despite the frequency of humanity's rejection of following him.

Questions to Consider while Reading

1. If God only creates and does good things, what is the purpose of the tree of knowledge of good and evil?

2. In what ways does sin affect the relationships among human beings in Gen 1–11?

3. Despite differences in response, is there any sense in which God's responses to sins are consistent?

Now Read: Gen 1–11

Creation and Goodness in the Garden

If you have not read Genesis before, you might have noticed something surprising in Gen 1–2: there appear to be two creation accounts. In Gen 1:1—2:3, we see the traditional six days of creation culminating in the creation of human beings in the image and likeness of God. Genesis 2:4–25 puts more emphasis on God creating Eve from Adam in order to form the human community. Both of these stories build up details demonstrating both the goodness of God as well as the fact that all of creation is there to support human beings.

We can think of the two creation accounts as looking at human nature from two equally important perspectives. The first account emphasizes the language of image and likeness. Genesis 1:26 states: "Then God said: Let us make human beings in our image, after our likeness." Many traditional interpretations focus on our abilities to reason and exercise free will as the explanation of how we human beings are created in God's image and likeness. This is a significant claim about what makes human beings distinct and what can be considered as necessary for our purpose. That we see God later interacting with his human children shows how these abilities are really geared towards saying "yes" or "no" to relationships. It is impossible to have the deepest and most meaningful relationships without having reason and free will. We will see that God's love for creation and God's desire that we be in loving relationships with him and each other shows up as the central message throughout both the Old Testament and the New Testament.

There is also a trinitarian element in this passage which has always been important to Christian interpreters. It builds on the purpose of having reason and free will. God says: "Let *us* make . . . " The plural form of the pronoun (as opposed to God saying "Let me make") has been explained in a number of ways. But for Christians, the text seems obviously to be implying that God the Father, God the Son, and God the Holy Spirit are making us in God's image and likeness. After all, Christianity does not believe that God was a singular person just waiting to start having relationships until after creating human beings. No. The one God, because God is Father, Son, and Holy Spirit, is by nature loving relationships. When God creates us in his image, he made a human nature which is geared biologically, socially, and spiritually to be in relationships. "Let us make" means that humans cannot be understood as solitary things.

This second element, the trinitarian one, also comes out in the second creation account through the emphasis on the marital unity between man and woman. Although God initially creates just a generic human in Gen 2, Jews and Christians have never understood the story of Eve's creation as some kind of afterthought, especially in light of the way Gen 1:26–27 puts the creation of man and woman together. In other words, the narrative which has God settle Adam in the Garden, has God state that Adam should have a suitable partner, and has God bring the animals for Adam to name is not interpreted as suggesting God needed to learn something. Rather, this all helps Adam to understand his own purpose and the purpose of human nature. When he finally meets Eve, Gen 2:23a tells us: "The man said: 'This one, at last, is bone of my bones and flesh of my flesh.'" The second account of creation then explains the fundamental role of marriage for human civilization. Genesis 2:24 states, "That is why a man leaves his father and mother and clings to his wife, and the two of them become one body." With these elements, Genesis presents the Garden as a place of harmony, love, relationships, goodness, and order.

Many people look at the world with all of its tragedy, dysfunction, and sin and ask: How could God have wanted this? Christianity has never begun with that question because Christianity is rooted in the truths of Gen 1–2. Its teaching about God as wholly good, as creating only good things, and as making humanity for the special purpose of loving relations is both theologically and philosophically sophisticated. But the story is only just beginning. The experience of all humans is not one of perfect harmony, love, and order. More of an explanation is necessary for the creation accounts in Gen 1–2 to make sense of all the bad things we do and all the bad we experience.

Sin: Disobedience, Lies, Murders, and all Evils

Sometimes, the snake is made to be the main actor in Gen 3. This leads some readers to mistakenly think that Genesis puts all the blame on the snake for Adam and Eve's sin and the expulsion from the Garden. This is not accurate. While bad influences are something we all experience in life, we all also know that a bad influence does not mean we can claim innocence after having followed that bad influence. Bad influences are destructive to relationships and personal growth, but they are not the final word on blame or consequences. The story of mankind's sin is primarily about the choices Adam and Eve make and the consequences of those choices.

Before moving forward, consider the tree of knowledge of good and evil (Gen 2:17), the only tree on which God put a restriction. Some people read Gen 1–3 thinking that God set Adam and Eve up to fail. Some also think that the tree of the knowledge of good and evil is an evil thing, and Adam and Eve became evil through contact with it. We have already seen though that such interpretations would violate the basic theological and philosophical beliefs of Christianity. God is perfectly good. And, God is a perfectly good and loving Creator. His intention could never have been for Adam and Eve to fail. Consider then the possibility that the tree was not the actual conveyor of evil knowledge but the one opportunity God gave humanity to grow in obedience. The story is saying that we learned about evil because we chose to bring it into the world through our disobedience. Another way of putting it is that the tree of knowledge of good and evil only revealed the evil in our disobedience; the story does not suggest that the tree either possessed or caused evil. In fact, this story provides the basis for the Christian teaching called original sin. Original sin does not simply refer to the sin of Adam and Eve as the first sin. It refers to the reality that by sinning, Adam and Eve caused a wound in our human nature. All human beings possess this condition of wounded human nature, not because God made us this way. We possess a wounded nature because we have been weakened in our souls and bodies because we chose to disobey God. The story which unfolds from here on out is the story of God addressing and correcting this corruption to our nature.

Notice how quickly sin spirals out of control. Adam and Eve chose to disobey God. The cause of this spiral was the pride of Eve and then Adam thinking that they could make themselves equal to God (Gen 3:5). Their pride made them lose sight of the nature of their relationship with God. It is a relationship which can only be in good order when they humbly and gratefully keep in mind that they were created by God out of love and depend on God for their existence. The consequence of their prideful disobedience was expulsion from the Garden. One way of interpreting this is that humanity expelled itself from God's presence. We see this in human relationships all of the time. Think, for example, of the number of times you have seen or experienced a friendship broken by conflict, deceit, or unfaithfulness. Perhaps that friendship was never repaired. Because Adam and Eve violated the harmony they had with God, the Garden, which physically and spiritually represents the unblemished relationship they originally had with God, no longer was a possible place for them to live.

The next story of Cain and Abel demonstrates a horrific deterioration in the first human family, worse than the sin of Adam and Eve. Out of jealousy Cain murders Abel. When God questions Cain about Abel's whereabouts, Cain ironically responds, "I do not know. Am I my brother's keeper?" (Gen 4:9). This insidious and lying response is ironic in the sense that the answer to Cain's question is "yes." Our purpose as human beings is, of course, to support and care for each other, to be each other's keepers as it were. Next, we see Lamech's prideful boast in the same chapter: "I have killed a man for wounding me, a young man for bruising me" (Gen 4:23). We have seen prideful disobedience, then a jealous murder attempted to be covered over with a lie, and now boastfulness about using murder to take revenge on having been wounded.

Finally, Genesis portrays humanity's embrace of endless sin and wickedness: "When the LORD saw how great the wickedness of human beings was on earth, and how every desire that their heart conceived was always nothing but evil, the LORD regretted making human beings on the earth, and his heart was grieved" (Gen 6:5–6). The Christian tradition typically does not interpret a text literally if such an interpretation cannot be supported logically. This passage is a good example. God is all-knowing and does not regret like human beings do after making bad decisions. Rather, this is a human portrayal of God meant to help the reader of Genesis comprehend how much the free will of human beings had been perverted and the extent to which they were rejecting good and holy relationships with each other and with God. The portrayal of nearly unbounded sin leads to the story of the Flood.

God's Responses to Sin as the Story Progresses

Genesis 1–11 presents complex topics through a quick succession of very diverse stories. Many of the elements in the stories are surprising and sometimes disturbing. For example, a very literal reading of the text would suggest that God walks in the Garden, that God is not all-knowing and needs to ask questions, and that God can experience surprise and regret. As noted already, such interpretations of the texts have typically been avoided because they do not do justice to God's nature as it is otherwise known and understood. That the details of the stories point to a main idea is the thing to keep in mind: the good God responds to human beings who repeatedly choose to use their gifts against the purpose God has given them. God gave free will and rationality for us to have relationships. Our poor use of these gifts in these diverse stories leads to instances of God's punishment, but they also give us evidence of God's patience.

We have seen how the expulsion from the Garden, for example, can be interpreted as simply another way of expressing the loss of the harmony, order, and fellowship with God. But the text also mentions the expulsion as God's action: "The Lord God therefore banished him from the garden of Eden, to till the ground from which he had been taken. He expelled the man, stationing the cherubim and the fiery revolving sword east of the garden of Eden, to guard the way to the tree of life" (Gen 3:23–24). We may have forgotten that the details of the story included, besides the tree of the knowledge of good and evil, another tree. This was the tree of life. We should pause for a moment if we want to jump at the conclusion that punishment is the reason for being barred from the tree. We can instead consider another idea Christians have had. God never intended us to live immortal lives with him in a corrupt state. Somehow, our first disobedience caused significant harm to the whole human family. As a result of human actions (those specifically of Adam and Eve), we are all caught up in the grip of sin. We all know that at times we look at sin and we say "yes" to it. We have been deeply wounded by sin, and we continue to be agents of sin in our own lives. Christians have often seen the expulsion from the Garden and the tree of life as the story demonstrating that God will never let us keep living in a corrupted state. The main point of the expulsion is that God will heal us so that we can share in truly good, holy, immortal life. Like many other times in our lives, healing often involves some pain.

Is a positive interpretation of the expulsion from the Garden consistent with God's punishing responses to sin in Gen 1–11? Yes, the stories do point to consistency. God did not take revenge upon Cain but rather put a mark on him so that he would not be killed by others he encountered (Gen 4:15). Perhaps this left open the possibility that Cain might come to regret and seek forgiveness for his horrific crime. Enoch (Gen 5:24) and Noah (Gen 6:9) are presented as uniquely righteous and thus afforded unique treatment. In the case of Enoch, he somehow is taken by God, and is traditionally understood to have gone straight to heaven. In the case of Noah, he and his family are responsible for repopulating the earth after God sends forth the Flood to deal with the story's emphasis on the total breakdown of human ethical standards. Note that the story of Noah, either before or after the flood, does not presume to say that Noah was without sin. The story seems to imply that Noah never lost his way into totally abandoning his relationship with God the way the rest of humanity at the time seems to have done. God responds by blessing Noah and his sons.

In addition to blessing Noah's family, the story shows God setting new conditions on the governance of the world. Genesis has already laid out the reason for these new guidelines. From the goodness of creation and the goodness of the Garden, Adam and Eve's choice to disobey led to uncontrolled sin and the necessity of the Flood. Human nature has been corrupted through this first act of rebellion, and human beings cannot return to their state by their own, now-corrupted wills. The **covenant** with Noah includes new elements of humanity's dominion over the earth and humanity's required respect for the lifeblood of animals (Gen 9:1–4). These features demonstrate that humanity's sin led to an obvious disharmony between human beings and the rest of creation. The ultimate act of relationship destruction (murder) is also now treated with the response of capital punishment: "Anyone who sheds the blood of a human being, by a human being shall that one's blood be shed; for in the image of God have human beings been made (Gen 9:6). This is an important passage indicating both the need to keep the worst forms of human sin in check as well as the assurance that our sins have not completely corrupted us. Evil certainly corrupts the good. But all that is in existence is good in that it is still God's creation.

Conclusion

Christianity looks unflinchingly at the sin and corruption in all people, in all societies, and in the fractured relationships between humanity and the world. The faith in a good God includes rejecting sin and corruption as God's will. The first eleven chapters of Genesis masterfully navigate the ability to believe in a good and perfect God and also this sin and corruption. When we look inside ourselves simultaneously at both the goodness and grandeur of human nature and also the shocking existence of corruption and sin, we can appreciate these themes.

A brief reflection on the story of the Tower of Babel in Gen 11 helps to demonstrate the human condition after the Flood. Some readers might be surprised at God's reaction to the building of the Tower based upon the rationale given in Gen 11:4: "Then they said, 'Come, let us build ourselves a city and a tower with its top in the sky, and so make a name for ourselves; otherwise we shall be scattered all over the earth." Traditional interpretations of this story saw a motivation based upon pride. This is similar to the pride of Adam and Eve and their desire to usurp God's rightful place in their lives. Even worse, many interpreters have seen in this text a motivation to build a tower to heaven in order to challenge or perhaps make war with God. God humbles these people in response by confusing their language. He breaks up their ability to work together. The Tower, when compared to the Garden story, shows an extreme level of contempt for God. God made us to thrive in human society by building relationships with each other and with him. The people in the land of Shinar attempted to use their relationships to reject and replace God. Such a use of free will can only bring corruption and misery.

Lastly, notice the importance of **genealogies** in Genesis, which are the lists of generations of families and tribes. The Bible often points to relationships as being at the heart of our human purpose. In addition to the relationships we create through marriage and friendship, Genesis emphasizes our relationships as tribes, nations, and the entire human family. These connections made through biology and choice will be seen repeatedly throughout the Bible's stories. It is in these relationships that human beings find their capacity to let God be in control of our futures. Genesis 1–11 is the beginning of the story of how God has loved us into existence, responds to us in our rebellion, and brings about the framework for our healing and redemption.

Study and Reflection Questions

1. What was surprising in your reading of Gen 1–11? Why?

2. Although the Christian tradition sees the good, loving, just, and merciful God at work in these chapters, why might some readers outside of Christianity (or Judaism) see a different portrait of God?

3. Aside from those elements mentioned in this chapter, what other elements point to God's nature as loving and God's activity as seeking our welfare?

3

Abraham and His Family

Preview

Genesis 12 begins a new stage of God's progressive actions
through history to bring salvation to humanity. The term
for this activity is "**salvation history**." In fact, God's interaction
with Abraham is the foundational event of salvation history for
the rest of the Bible as well as history itself. God chooses Abraham
(originally called Abram) and his wife Sarah (originally called
Sarai) to be the start of the people known as the Jews. This same
family is also known as the "Hebrews" prior to the Exodus and
the "Israelites" after. They come to be called "Israel" because God
gives the name "Israel" to Jacob, Abraham's grandson. They come
to be called "Judahites" because they belonged to the Kingdom of
Judah, with "Jew" coming as a later development from this last
term. Regardless of name, the Jews are a nation of people connected by bloodline. This is a central idea to keep in mind as we
read through the history of the Jews from Gen 12 and into the
New Testament. (In order to emphasize the reality of the continuity of the **covenant** people beginning with Abraham, this book
will anachronistically use the words "Jew" and "Jewish," despite
the historically more accurate progression of using "Hebrews,"
"Israelites," "Judahites," and then "Jews.") It might seem odd at
first that God chooses to work so intimately with one particular
people. However, salvation history is about that special relationship blossoming over time to include all human beings. This

movement also helps us appreciate how God uses an invitation to obey him, first with the Jews and then with all others, as opposed to forcing people into obedience with divine power. We can note then that the movement of salvation is the movement of God developing loving and obedient relationships.

The stories in Gen 12–50 primarily cover four generations. First, God makes a special covenant with Abraham and his wife Sarah. They have Isaac who marries Rebekah. This second generation produces twins, named Jacob and Esau. The covenant travels specifically to Jacob who in turn marries two sisters named Leah and Rachel. Through Leah, Rachel, and two concubines named Zilpah and Bilhah, Jacob has twelve sons. As will be seen in our reading of Genesis, these twelve sons and their respective clans represent what comes to be understood as the twelve tribes of Israel. More than a few of these stories about Abraham, Isaac, Jacob, and Jacob's twelve sons are familiar to people other than Jews and Christians. However, the importance of these figures in the history of God's plan for the salvation of all human beings through Abraham and Sarah cannot be overestimated.

Before encountering some of these stories, readers should be aware of the fact that biblical figures are human beings who sometimes make bad decisions or immoral ones. This surprises, confuses, or otherwise discourages some new readers of the Bible. Many people assume they will only find stories of saints doing saintly things when they open the Scriptures. But, the Bible witnesses to men and women who are called to righteousness and holiness (like all people are) and who fall short at times. The Bible's inspired nature also gives us insights into God's perceptions of people and events. These insights can be surprising. For example, readers might find the sins of certain biblical figures, such as King David, as being wildly extreme and almost unforgivable. How many people do you know who have committed adultery and then murdered the spouse to hide the sin (2 Sam 11)? At the same time, the text also speaks about God's love for David and even about David's unparalleled faith. Such an example alerts us to the fact that much more is going on in the lives of these figures than these stories relay. This can include the quality and extent of David's humility and repentance, which allows God to work in the repentant David's life. Every element in a biblical story and sometimes the stories as a whole are not supposed to present the best example of faith and holiness. These stories show how a wide variety of human beings, in a variety of circumstances, behave in response to the enormous responsibility of trying to understand and follow God's will.

Questions to Consider while Reading:

1. In what ways do you see God acting with a specific person or group as showing something about his love for all people?

2. What elements of the text of Gen 22 stand out as surprising or confusing? Why?

3. How does the story of Joseph and his brothers point to the complicated relationship between the activities of both God and human beings?

Now Read: Gen 12–15; 22; 37–50

The Covenant with Abraham

The word "covenant" can mean a pledge, alliance, or contract. In its biblical usage connecting God to the Jews, it contains a deep sense of God's insistence that he established a relationship which will endure and on which he will not turn his back. We already encountered this word used repeatedly in regard to God's promise in Gen 9. There God vowed to never destroy the earth and its inhabitants again with a flood, saying, "This is the sign of the covenant that I am making between me and you and every living creature with you for all ages to come: I set my bow in the clouds to serve as a sign of the covenant between me and the earth" (Gen 9:12–13). When considering the covenant made with Abraham, it is helpful to recognize that the covenant promising protection from another flood does not depend on the actions of people.

God makes a promise to Noah and all of creation which simply entails his promise to not act in a certain way. In the covenant with Abraham, we see that God has expectations for the Jews in addition to his promises.

In Gen 12, God reveals the promise he makes to Abraham and the basic dimensions of the covenant, which he explains in later chapters. But Gen 12 is singularly important for its clarity about the scope and purpose of this special covenant with the Jewish people. With no prior communication between God and Abraham given in the text, God speaks these words:

> The Lord said to Abram: Go forth from your land, your relatives, and from your father's house to a land that I will show you. I will make of you a great nation, and I will bless you; I will make your name great, so that you will be a blessing. I will bless those who bless you and curse those who curse you. All the families of the earth will find blessing in you. (Gen 12:1–3)

There are three parts in God's promise to Abraham. Each one of them is central to the entire story of the Bible which culminates in the work of Jesus Christ.

The first part of the promise is land. God seeks Abraham's obedience in that he directs Abraham to a land of blessing. God has a gift for Abraham, and Abraham's responsibility for receiving that blessing is the travel involved. This is not a small thing in a world in which safety and stability was tied to family and clan relationships. To depart for a new land is a supreme act of trust on Abraham's part in that such a response puts one's life in the hands of God. It is helpful to compare this kind of response to that of Adam and Eve, who already possessed the blessing of a special place to live and the blessing of communion with God himself in that place in a special way. Though living richly and abundantly, Adam and Eve responded with rebellion to God's simple commandment to not eat of one tree. Abraham and Sarah, on the other hand, respond to God in humility and trust. These twin dispositions can be classified as central themes throughout the Bible in terms of its emphasis on how human beings must relate to God. Abraham and Sarah's departure under God's care for this promised land shows just how human beings should choose to respond to God's instruction.

The second part of the promise is a large family which will grow into a nation. Many people are familiar with the phrase *"chosen people"* in reference to the Jews. Here we are seeing the meaning behind the beginnings of this phrase. It points to the fact that God reached into history and selected one particular man and woman, Abraham and Sarah, with whom to have a special relationship. We can also identify the element of God's concern for people with this second part of the promise. So far, we have seen a pattern in God's interaction with human beings, and that pattern is characterized by interacting with humanity mostly in family groups. God knew it was not good for Adam to live alone, so he made Eve. Adam and Eve are physically equipped to make a larger family, so they do. When humanity sins and Noah finds favor with God for being good, it is Noah's family which is saved. The Bible's repeated **genealogies**, those long lists of family connections, also point to the reality that we find our identity and purpose through each other. We will see again and again that God blesses and redeems communities, or he redeems individuals who in turn bring that redeeming experience to share in communities.

The third part of the promise is perhaps the most surprising. Although Gen 12 begins the rest of the Bible's historical focus on the growth and development of the Jewish people specifically, the third part of the promise has a universal scope. God indeed made a covenant with the chosen people, the Jews, in order to allow them to live uniquely in obedience to him. Nevertheless, we can also see that God binds the entire human race into his promise to the Jewish people. Without giving any details or offering any explanation, God promises that blessings and curses flow to all human beings from the response they give to God's work with the Jews.

God's Test of Abraham

Genesis 22 includes a strange and seemingly horrific test of Abraham. God commands the following: "Take your son Isaac, your only one, whom you love, and go to the land of Moriah. There offer him up as a burnt offering on one of the heights that I will point out to you" (Gen 22:2). With relatively few words, three elements to this command seemingly contradict the portrait of God so far painted in the preceding chapters of Genesis. First, it appears that God is going back on his word. God promised in Gen 17:18 that a great nation will come through Isaac. How can this be if God orders Isaac's death? Second, how can God command a loving father to murder his own beloved child? Such a commandment seems like a monstrous reversal from God's own condemnation of murder set out in Gen 9:5–6. Finally, how is it that God would want the murder of an innocent? Previously, God was shown as punishing those who harm innocent people.

Our understanding of **general revelation** and **special revelation** can be helpful in deepening our reading of Gen 22. The objections noted above to the three major elements of the story about God's command to sacrifice Isaac would fit into the category of general revelation. People do not need a special revelation from God to know that breaking promises, violating the love and duty we have to loved ones, and harming innocent people are all morally wrong. That God spoke to Abraham and gave a specific command to sacrifice means that this interaction with Abraham counts as special revelation. Before we try to interpret the text, it is most important to reemphasize the Christian assertion that general revelation and special revelation can never really be at odds with each other. God is the source of all revelation and all knowledge. Therefore, Christians do not look at this passage and believe that God is really immoral or that he really commands immorality. There is something deeper going on here.

One primary way of interpreting the purpose of Gen 22 is as a test of trust. God is asking for Abraham's obedience, which we will recall was the element lacking in Adam and Eve's response to God's command back in the Garden. Gen 22 does not tell us about the mental and spiritual war that must have been going on in Abraham's head and heart. Rather, the author simply tells the story with an emphasis on obedience, implicitly emphasizing the idea of Abraham's trust in God. What would he trust though? Abraham knows God's promise to keep the **covenant** by which the descendants through Isaac will surpass the countable stars in that deep, black, desert sky. We might then suspect that Abraham's trust is in God's ability to either save Isaac by changing the command or by bringing him back to life. In either case, Abraham would know that all of the aspects which seem contradictory, unjust, or evil, must themselves not be the real nature of the command or the outcome.

Abraham's faithfulness is proven by his willingness to comply, but Christianity does not teach that the nature of faith is to be found in God commanding us to do immoral things. Another way of putting it would be to say that the Scriptures certainly do not teach that faith is to be acted out like a young member in a gang, mafia family, or cartel who is ordered to do something evil to prove loyalty to the group. Who would want to worship such a God? The faithfulness of Abraham is good because it is rooted in an obedience to listen to God and act on his command, trusting that good must be at the heart of the command and the act. Otherwise, general and special revelation would be at odds, ultimately making God a sort of incoherent and horrible dictator.

The deepest meaning of the text in the Christian tradition is a spiritual reading in which Jesus and his life are seen through the events with Isaac. In theology, this is called "**typology**." It is the term describing one event or person in the Scriptures as foreshadowing or being a kind of model of something or someone later in the text. Christians mostly see in the Old Testament typological elements pointing to Jesus himself, and this kind of reading is based upon Jesus' own words. In Luke's Gospel, Jesus teaches his disciples this very methodology when he was surprised by their inability to understand his death and predicted resurrection:

> And he said to them, "Oh, how foolish you are! How slow
> of heart to believe all that the prophets spoke! Was it not
> necessary that the Messiah should suffer these things and
> enter into his glory?" Then beginning with Moses and
> all the prophets, he interpreted to them what referred to
> him in all the scriptures. (Luke 24:25–27)

In Judaism, the traditional belief was that Moses wrote Genesis, Exodus, Leviticus, Numbers, and Deuteronomy. This makes the Genesis story about the testing of Abraham and the command to sacrifice Isaac reasonably understood by Christians as a **type** of Jesus' life and death. The spiritual meaning of this story about Abraham's testing is bound up with John 3:16, which we will recall from the beginning of chapter 1. One common element of these connections is found in the Christian understanding of the title "**Christ**." This title is the Greek form of the Hebrew word "**Messiah**." Both "Christ" and "Messiah" mean "anointed one." This is the title of the person spoken of by the Jewish prophets who would be sent by God to bring salvation and victory to the Jewish people.

Consider the understanding that this text about Abraham's testing gives us a window into God the Father and God the Son's experience of sacrifice for humanity's benefit. After all, God does not actually ask Abraham to go through with this unjust sacrifice. But God himself, as Jesus, does in fact faithfully experience his own sacrifice for the sins of humanity, and therefore for the sake of humanity's healing. Abraham's faithful obedience is elevated in a spiritual interpretation. In this reading, God the Father and God the Son jointly offer the sacrifice both knowingly and willingly. The faithfulness involved is primarily about the faithfulness of God to do whatever is necessary for the healing of the world. As is taught in the New Testament, that necessary thing is God's own death and resurrection. When we get to the Gospel stories about Jesus, we will be able to compare the groundwork of the ideas laid down here with those in the Gospels by Matthew and John.

Joseph, His Visions, and His Brothers

Joseph and his brothers are the great grandchildren of Abraham and Sarah. Their story and the growth of the Jewish people is bound up, among other things, in faithfulness, pride, hatred, jealousy, mercy, and the ability of God to work in the hearts and lives of imperfect people. One feature of the family dynamics among the sons of Jacob is a kind of favoritism which helps fuel the conflict in the story. Genesis 37:3–4 states: "Israel (Jacob) loved Joseph best of all his sons, for he was the child of his old age; and he had made him a long ornamented tunic. When his brothers saw that their father loved him best of all his brothers, they hated him so much that they could not say a kind word to him." Most parents understand the dangers of favoritism, but Jacob appears to be oblivious. This factor helps to set the hearts of Joseph's brothers against him.

Genesis 37 also includes the supernatural element of Joseph's dreams. These dreams are not specifically identified as messages from God early in the story. However, it becomes clear through the experiences of the family that Joseph's dreams and his ability to interpret dreams are gifts from God which ultimately work to save the whole family. In Gen 37, Joseph tells his family about two dreams he has had, and the family is insulted. His dreams seem to indicate his superior position at the head of the family. Perhaps most interesting in these stories is Jacob's own chastisement of Joseph, who skeptically asks in vs. 10, "Can it be that I and your mother and your brothers are to come and bow to the ground before you?" Neither Joseph, his father, nor his brothers know that these dreams are messages from God which do indeed predict the family's future situation.

We know from our reading of Genesis that the story of Joseph's rise to power comes through his brothers' hatred and betrayal. Joseph himself, after he has become second in Egypt only to Pharaoh, has the greatest insight about his life's purpose. When he eventually reveals his true identity to his brothers, Joseph says, "But now do not be distressed, and do not be angry with yourselves for having sold me here. It was really for the sake of saving lives that God sent me here ahead of you" (Gen 45:5). An understanding of God's activity in these episodes is something of which Jacob's children seem to have not been aware. What are we to make, however, of the brothers' turn to murderous violence early in Joseph's life. Notice that later in life, Joseph is not claiming that God made his brothers turn to him with hatred and violence. As we have seen already, God neither commands or encourages evil. Perhaps, we might suggest that if God had any active part to play in the murderous attempt on Joseph's life it was in helping Reuben feel the obligation to protect Joseph from injustice (Gen 37:21–22; 29–30). In all cases, we can say that the brothers' violence and injustice against Joseph, sparked by God's gift of dreams, was a complicated feature in the lives of Jacob's family. Furthermore, we can follow Joseph's understanding that God brought good even from evil intentions and actions.

Joseph's dreams and his ability to interpret dreams were neither the only, nor the primary, gifts given to him by God. The powerful interaction with dreams really came from Joseph's humility and trust in God. The Bible identifies Joseph's blessings with the fact that God stayed with him. This in turn led to blessings for those around him, such as the blessings which came to his master Potiphar's house. But Joseph's righteousness in rejecting the sexual advances of Potiphar's wife (Gen 39:7–12) relied directly on his understanding of justice and his service to God. Joseph asks Potiphar's wife in Gen 39:9: "He (Potiphar) has withheld from me nothing but you, since you are his wife. How, then, could I do this great wrong and sin against God?" When sent to jail, Genesis tells us that God stayed with Joseph and brought him prosperity there as well. Again, we see dreams enter the story, but Joseph specifically puts God's power at the center of his interpretation. Asking the imprisoned cupbearer and baker about their dreams, Joseph states: "'Why do you look so troubled today?' They answered him, 'We have had dreams, but there is no one to interpret them.' Joseph said to them, 'Do interpretations not come from God? Please tell me the dreams'" (Gen 40:7–8). This part of the story includes Joseph telling the cupbearer good news and simply asking that the man remember him when his fortunes have improved.

Although two years had to pass before the cupbearer remembered Joseph, the Pharaoh's anguish over unexplained dreams finally became the situation by which Joseph's original dreams could come to fruition. Joseph successfully interprets Pharaoh's dreams with God's help. Joseph shows both the power of God's knowledge and also that God blesses those who are humble and obedient. Joseph's humility and trust in God leads directly to his dramatic rise in station from youngest child, to slave, to prisoner, and then to second in charge of Egypt. Perhaps most important about the dreams of Joseph from the beginning of his story to their coming to pass is the family's misinterpretation of the dreams' true purpose. The incorrect interpretation which enraged them all was the idea of Joseph's power and status over them. The true understanding of the dreams was in the ability of Joseph to use all of the power he had come to possess to bring blessings to his family. These blessings will be relevant not only for his immediate family, but for all future generations.

Conclusion

The stories of Abraham and his family witness to the variety of ways in which God communicates with human beings. We saw the way in which God spoke specifically to Abraham in the form of a promise, one which would bring not only blessings to his family but also blessings to all the peoples of the world. We saw the complicated way in which God specifically tested Abraham to emphasize the importance of family and to act as a foreshadowing of Jesus' sacrifice on the cross. The outcome of that story was in fact a testing of Abraham's love and trust as well as a clear typology of the sacrifice God the Father and God the Son made. Finally, we have the instance of God communicating to Joseph through dreams and their interpretation. In this last case, Joseph's story reveals that he himself did not really understand what God was communicating until his life had been fully formed in obedience, trust, and love of God. Only at the height of his worldly powers could he see that God lovingly shaped his journey for the protection and service of his family.

The story of God's **chosen people** only makes sense in light of the scriptural witness to God's interactions with the Jewish people over the course of centuries. In the next chapter, we will look at the story of God's acts of mercy and protection for Jacob and his family as they face suffering and slavery. Though Genesis ends with Joseph's death and the security of his family, his final request points to his understanding that the Jews were never meant to remain in Egypt. Near the point of his death, Joseph acknowledges this as well as his trust that God would eventually bring the family back to the promised land:

> Joseph said to his brothers: "I am about to die. God will surely take care of you and lead you up from this land to the land that he promised on oath to Abraham, Isaac, and Jacob." Then, putting the sons of Israel under oath, he continued, "When God thus takes care of you, you must bring my bones up from this place." (Gen 50:24–25)

Joseph's story is one in which God's care, protection, and love remains at the center, despite such hardships as familial betrayal, slavery, and prison. Although God is never said to have spoken to Joseph as he had to Abraham and Jacob, we as readers might consider the idea that Genesis is presenting the clarity of God's loving communication through Joseph's story as a lesson to us all about the ways in which God might be speaking to us.

Study and Reflection Questions:

1. What detail or story from this chapter's readings seems to connect with God's actions in the readings from Gen 1–11?

2. What aspect of the text was most challenging to the idea that love is at the center of who God is and what God does? Why?

3. In what ways do these selections from Genesis teach us how to love God and each other?

4

The Exodus, Torah, Temple, and Prophecy

Preview

The Biblical selections associated with this chapter look at a broad sweep of Jewish history. Many Christians are unfamiliar with the general story of the Jewish people. This means that many Christians remain unfamiliar with the way the Word continued to interact with humanity to prepare us for his **Incarnation**. It was, of course, God's self-expression and guidance of the nation of Israel which directly prepared the way for God's own climactic coming to his people as Jesus. The Biblical selections for this chapter span the events of the Exodus, the giving of the Torah, the settling of the Holy Land, the building of the Temple, and an example of God's work among the prophets through the example of Jonah.

The Jews began to prosper in Egypt after the time of Joseph. Then a new line of Pharaohs came to power and were threatened by the Jewish presence. They enslaved and oppressed the Jews. Moses was a Jew raised in the house of Pharaoh, but he ran away from Egypt after killing an Egyptian in defense of a fellow Jew. After living for years in exile, Moses heard God speak from the burning bush. God commanded Moses to go and rescue his People from the oppression of the Egyptians so that they could worship. The rest of the book of Exodus includes Moses going back to Egypt and bringing a series of plagues upon the Egyptians. Miraculously, God, through Moses, leads the Jews into the desert where they travel to

Mount Sinai to receive the **Ten Commandments** as well as the rest of the **Torah**, which is sometimes translated "Law" or "Instruction." The Torah renews God's promise and gives a comprehensive guide to living for the Jews. It is intended to support the loving relationship between the people with God and with each other.

When the Jews finally returned to the land promised to Abraham (i.e. "The Promised Land"), they settled in different areas based upon tribes. You will recall that the Jewish people all come through Jacob and, therefore, his twelve sons. This period of Jewish history, called the time of the judges, involves repeated examples of what Biblical scholars often refer to as the cycle of sin and redemption. The judges were leaders raised up by God to fight against foreign nations hostile to the Israelites and then particular groups of the Jews. This is a period in which the tribes are not united by a single government. The stories we will read from the book of Judges point to a new period in Jewish history and a new way in which God interacts with his people.

The selection from First Kings might seem odd for a study such as this. It describes, however, a critical moment in the history of the Jewish people: the building and dedication of the **Temple** in Jerusalem. After the period of the Judges, the Jews demanded that God give them a king like other nations. Despite God telling the people that it would be better if he alone remained their heavenly King without a human king, the people continued to ask for a human king. Before King Solomon, the builder of the Temple, there was first King Saul (an unrighteous king) and then King David (a righteous king, though with a personal history that involved a few particularly shocking sins). David's son Solomon built the Temple according to God's instructions. In addition to the giving of the Torah by which the Jews would know how to live their daily lives, God also gave the Jewish nation a Temple which would be a place of God's special presence. First Kings 6–9 provides a wonderful summary of the care and specificity that went into the building of the Temple as well as a theological understanding of what the Temple's building meant for the nation in terms of its relationship with God.

Finally, the book of Jonah represents a brief, but often already well-known, story of a prophet. This book is understood by many Jews and Christians to likely be more of a religious fable telling us about God's love for all human beings rather than a necessarily historical report of a prophet's work. Jonah's story allows us to consider how God is understood to be speaking to human beings through the work of special figures called prophets. In the story, Jonah is sent to a foreign nation, a nation which was an *enemy* of the Jews. The work of the other prophets known in Jewish history, by and large and by contrast with Jonah, was that of encouraging the Jewish people or condemning them for having abandoned the **covenant**. As already seen, the covenant included responsibilities directly tied to living a holy life through obedience to the Torah and worship of God at the Temple of Jerusalem. But Jonah is different. Jonah's story is one about a prophet of God being sent to a foreign nation in order to demand that they repent of their sins. His message does not include asking the Ninevites to convert to Judaism. Rather, it is one in which God chooses to tell non-Jews that their ways are harmful to themselves and to call them to a life of righteousness. In the Jewish tradition, the word used for everyone who is not a Jew is "**Gentile**," coming from the word meaning "nations." The message of Jonah highlights the fact that God never left the Gentile world entirely in the dark or separated from his words and actions of love and forgiveness.

Questions to Consider while Reading

1. How do the events of Exodus help us make sense of the Ten Commandments?

2. What aspects in the selection of Judges do you see as connected to aspects read in Genesis or Exodus?

3. How do the themes of obedience and holiness stand out in these readings?

Now Read: Exod 1–15; 19–20; Deut 5–6;
Judg 2–4; 1 Kgs 6:1—9:9; Jonah

Exodus and Deuteronomy as Salvation and Sacred Living

The word "exodus" means "a going out," as in a mass emigration. As noted, the Exodus refers to the event in which God sent Moses to lead God's People out of the slavery and oppression in Egypt to liberation in the Promised Land. This is the event in which God both speaks and acts in order to end the violence and injustice being done to the Jews. For this reason, the Jewish tradition looks at the Exodus as the primary historical event demonstrating God's love of the Jews and his decisive action to bring an end to all of the evils associated with the Jews' enslavement. Furthermore, Exodus is also read as a significant witness to God's desire and will to act in all of our lives to liberate us from slavery of any sort. We will see later in the book that Christians view the Exodus both historically and typologically. It is all those things Jewish tradition sees in it, but it is also a **type** of the liberation humanity gains through Jesus Christ's death and **resurrection**. In this reading, the slavery of the Jews is seen as a great evil from which God wants to, and does, liberate the Jews. But complete liberation of human beings can only come when we are all liberated from sin and death. This is the liberation which Jesus brings and which the Exodus points to typologically. Therefore, the spiritual meaning of Exodus for Christianity cannot be separated from Christ's death and resurrection.

God's commission to Moses occurs at the burning bush in Exod 3. God reveals to Moses that he has heard the cry of his People. God also reveals his name. This name is given in the Hebrew text as YHWH and is called the **Tetragrammaton**, meaning "four letters." It is usually given in English as **Yahweh**. The meaning of this name is something like "I am who I am," and it indicates God's nature as the only truly existing thing. The Jewish and Christian traditions understand the implicit idea that this name affirms that everything other than God depends for existence on him. The Jewish tradition eventually comes to avoid saying and writing this name because of its special sacredness; in so doing, this practice is seen as honoring the intimacy God is willing to share with his people. Most important in this example of **special revelation** is the fact that God is telling Moses and the rest of the Jews information about himself. As we all know, sharing thoughts, ideas, and information about ourselves is exactly how we deepen our relationships with each other. God shows us that our relationship is the same with him. If we want to get closer to him, we must listen to what he tells us about himself.

God's very active participation in the Exodus story demonstrates time and again the hallmarks of special revelation. Between God's direct call to Moses, the plagues sent because of Pharaoh's obstinacy, and the leading of the people out of Egypt with columns of fire and cloud, God shows consistency in the actions necessary to bring about the freedom of the Jews. But the 10 plagues seem to some readers as either particularly harsh or too broadly applied, leading to innocent suffering. This is a very good part of Scripture on which to dwell and consider a few ideas central to Christianity. First, recall that Christians affirm that general and special revelation will always coincide because God is perfectly just, merciful, and loving. As difficult as these passages might be, Christian interpreters have always affirmed that God's perfect justice, mercy, and love must stand behind the events portrayed. Think, for example, of Pharaoh's heart being hardened. Pharaoh is the one person who can listen to God and free the Jews, yet the text tells us repeatedly about Pharaoh being obstinate and hardening his heart, as well as God hardening Pharaoh's heart (Exod 9:12). Because Christians don't believe that God would force anyone to act in certain ways (especially evil ones!) it is traditional to read the text with more nuance. It was God's demand for Pharaoh to act rightly which became the very thing that hardened Pharaoh's heart. Consider the times in your life when you were told the right thing to do, and you chose to do the opposite especially because you did not want to listen.

Second, we must connect all God's words and actions to help make a complete picture of the situation. Although Pharaoh is king and is ultimately responsible for the actions of Egypt, the Bible speaks of God judging nations. Consider, for example, the situation of people willingly following and supporting unjust or evil leaders. In such situations, everyone involved finds a way to participate in injustice and sin, even if to a smaller degree. Consider also the basic Christian idea that all are sinners. It is sometimes easy to think of divine justice as similar to human justice. If I beat and rob someone, it might be proven that I have done one of those things, but not both those things. In terms of human justice, and our critically important principle of "innocent until proven guilty," it would be unjust to punish me for the thing it could not be proved I did. But this is not the justice of God. Christians worship God specifically because God will only ever act in perfect justice. In those times where we might not be able to see causes and effects of sin and punishment, Christians continue to affirm that God has complete and perfect information and never acts unjustly.

Exodus 20 tells of the giving of the Ten Commandments. Many people mistakenly believe that these commandments are the whole Torah. Instead, the Ten Commandments function as a summary of basic duties everyone owes to God (these are the first three found in Exod 20:2–11) and basic duties everyone owes to other people (these are the next seven commandments found in Exod 20:12–17). These commandments were written by God on stone tablets and were kept in the Ark of the Covenant. The Catholic tradition recognizes these commandments as summarizing the far more particular instructions found in the Torah. The book of Deuteronomy repeats these ten and, like the books of Leviticus and Numbers, gives many more. In fact, Jewish tradition counts 613 positive and negative commands in the Torah which map out how Jews must live. However, Deut 6:4–9 provides the great declaration of faith (called the **Shema**) recited daily by many Jews to this day. It begins: "Hear, O Israel! The LORD is our God, the LORD alone! Therefore, you shall love the LORD, your God, with your whole heart, and with your whole being, and with your whole strength" (Deut 6:4–5). Both the Ten Commandments and the Shema summarize what the whole Torah is about for the Jews. It is about the

Jews receiving God's instructions for how to live a sacred life. This sacred life of living according to Torah is one devoted to loving God and neighbor daily as the heart of true worship.

The Cycle of Sin and Redemption

When the Jews settled in the Promised Land, there were many other tribes and nations present. Conflicts and wars ensued between the peoples already there and the newly arrived Jews, who were commanded by God to take possession of the land. The stories in Judges present a pattern of Jewish faithlessness, God's judgment, and God's forgiveness. The cycle of sin and redemption refers to the repetitious experiences as exemplified in the book of Judges. The cycle begins with groups of Jews turning to other gods and abandoning their **covenant** with God. Although the Torah (which includes the Ten Commandments) offers the Jewish people an outline for living sacred lives, it begins by commanding faithfulness and complete devotion to the one true God. Recall Exod 20:3: "You shall not have other gods beside me." God, therefore, responds to this unfaithfulness by allowing other nations to oppress the Jews. The Jews cry out in the misery of their oppression and ask for God to save them. God raises up a judge from among the people, a military ruler. This judge leads the people in battle and successfully brings liberation to the Jews. The Jewish people gratefully thank God, settle back into their land, and then proceed to turn their backs on God and the covenant again. Thus, the cycle begins anew.

Many readers are at first aghast at the faithlessness of the Jewish people in this book. They ask questions like the following:

- How can the Jews have turned their backs on God when God had rescued them from Egypt?

- How can they have started to worship other gods when the Torah is clear about the need for faithfulness?

- How can they have begun to live holy lives through the Torah and lives of safety through God's protection and just cast these things aside?

These are all good questions. But, a bad reading of the text concludes that the Jews are uniquely unfaithful. A good reading of the text begins with our own hearts and our own experiences. When reading Judges, it is good for a believer in God to ask: how many times have I turned my back on God? The point of such a question is not to lead to excuses for the Jews during the time of the Judges, nor for ourselves. It is to help us understand the fact that sin pervades every human life, and a desire to stop sinning does not lead to the ability to stop all sinning. This idea can be found throughout the Old Testament and is the basis for understanding why it is that God himself came as Jesus to die and rise in order to defeat sin and death in a way we cannot.

In our own times, being respectful of other's religions and traditions seems both natural and just. It can be confusing to see God judging other religions and practices so harshly. A few things need to be kept in mind both about the practices of some of these ancient religions as well as the biblical understanding of faithfulness to the covenant. First, the ancient gods mentioned in Judges and the Old Testament include Baal and Astarte, among others. These gods were associated with such practices as child sacrifice, sexual immorality, and magic. Dabbling in allegiance to these gods meant that the Jews were turning to sinful practices. We recall that the Torah details a way for the Jews to live in holiness and unity with God. The giving of the Torah is a central element to fulfillment of God's promise that Abraham's descendants would be a light for all nations. By forsaking the gift of Torah, the Jewish people also were forsaking a healthy and holy life empowered by God's loving attention.

Second, the Jewish understanding of remaining faithful to the covenant involves being true to the Person who is Creator and lord of all life. This is the opposite of how some people think about obedience. There can be a tendency among some to think about following God's laws as if they are just made up, arbitrary commands or as if they are burdensome. Judaism and Christianity reject this kind of thinking. Instead, Christianity and Judaism see God's commandments as the means by which we can live our best and fullest lives. This thinking comes from the belief that God's commandments are rooted in his very nature, and because we are created by God, they are rooted in our nature also. God is the very definition of existence, and he is just, holy, merciful, and loving. God made us with the ability to enjoy life with him and this means living as he is. In the ancient world, religions typically did not think of the gods and goddesses as perfectly just, holy, merciful, and loving. Instead, these figures were seen as sources of power and protection for human beings who appeased them. They were not thought of as the only true reality upon which all creation existed, as the Jews understood Yahweh. This is why Christians and Jews think of obedience to God's commands as the ability to live our lives most richly and to the fullest.

Communication with God through the Temple and Prophets

The dedication of the Jerusalem **Temple** by King Solomon reminds us that the relationship with God and direct communion with him stands at the center of the Jewish experience. We have so far seen the importance of the **Torah's** role in guiding the people toward actions which promote the Jewish people's relationship with God and each other. The Temple, however, was the special place through which the Jew could most directly and personally encounter God. We might compare these elements of Torah and Temple to family life. Torah is essentially like the rules and expectations of behavior which a good father and mother set for their children. The Temple is like the time spent together, such as family meals.

Notice that in this analogy of family life, both aspects of family rules and family time balance each other. Rules in a loving household are never just made-up commands to follow, as if they have no other purpose than to annoy some members of the family. That is pretty frequently the perception children have of their parents' rules. But good parents do not make up house rules this way. Good parents try to create a framework by which love, respect, self-sacrifice, and the shared duties of maintaining the home are expressed. When a household has a shared framework for acceptable behaviors and language, then family time is made easier and better. Families find that they can support and strengthen each member when everyone knows what is expected. This promotes better relationships, and it also provides an inherent framework for reconciling after the fights which are inevitable in all relationships. The Torah and Temple act in similar ways for the Jewish people to live with each other and for the Jewish people, individually and collectively, to be in communion with God.

First Kings 6–7 provides a detailed description of the Temple's building. Some readers might find the details seemingly boring or perhaps irrelevant, like the genealogical lists found in the Scriptures. Consider though the place of the Temple for Jews. It is a sacred and holy place of God's presence. On the one hand, we can think that seeing all the details of construction added majesty to the experience of those Jews who worshipped at the Temple. On the other, we might also assume that knowing the details of the construction of the entire building (parts of which only the priests saw) acted in a way to diminish any sense worship at the Temple was magic. Both Judaism and Christianity are rooted in a clear-sighted relationship with God rather than the magic-oriented religious practices of the ancient world. The Temple is not a place of magical mystery. It is a place of meeting between the Lord God of the world and his **chosen people**.

The dedicatory words of Solomon starting at the beginning of 1 Kgs 8 point to important ideas about the relationship of the Jewish people with God and the purpose of the Temple. Notice that the people are not to think of God being confined in the holy place (1 Kgs 8:27), but also notice that this Temple is understood as a place God participates with the people in a special way (1 Kgs 8:10–13). Additionally, a major element of Solomon's dedication points to the Temple's role as the single most important place by which the people can receive forgiveness for their sins. The Torah provides the Jewish people with instructions on how to live holy and righteous lives. The Temple included the purpose of being the place to receive forgiveness through animal sacrifice. Since the

Garden, humanity has known that sin leads to separation from God, and separation from God leads to death.

Animal sacrifice involved all or part of the animal being burned for the forgiveness of sins in recognition that sin brings the loss of life. Jewish tradition in general acknowledges the symbolic value of an animal's death as a replacement for the death we bring on ourselves by our sins. The Christian tradition acknowledges the important role the Temple and its sacrificial system could play in uniting the Jews to God and helping conform their hearts to his commands. But the Christian tradition also proclaims the typological importance in the Temple and its sacrificial system as culminating in God's own death on the cross. As will be discussed in later chapters, it is God's own death on the cross as the man Jesus which truly can bring about effective forgiveness and healing.

Finally, this chapter turns to the prophet Jonah. Many read this book in light of the obvious humor involved. This is the tale of a surprisingly non-compliant prophet, and the elements of Jonah's disobedience and complaints are enough to surprise even children. Along with the elements of humor, there are also extremely important theological ideas. The story's conclusion, for example, points to this prophet's entirely misplaced priorities and callousness. God reproaches Jonah for his concern for a plant and not for the more than 120,000 people who need humility and forgiveness in their lives (Jonah 4:10–11). But another important element revealed by the prophet is that of God's care for all human beings. This prophet is sent by God to the enemies of Israel because these people "cannot know their right hand from their left" (Jonah 4:11). That is to say, these people had lost any clarity about the moral demands they should have been aware of by virtue of being created in God's image and likeness. God therefore addressed the Ninevites with the **special revelation** in the work of Jonah when the Ninevites had failed to engage effectively with their ability to know right from wrong through **general revelation**.

Conclusion

The variety of the biblical selections read for this chapter demonstrates a deep interrelationship in the history and writings of the Jewish people regarding God's love of people, his actions to bring redemption to them, his actions to provide a guide for holy living, and his actions to provide a framework for forgiveness. Although most of the stories concern God's interactions with the Jewish people, the book of Jonah clearly shows God acting to bring redemption and healing to the **Gentiles**. Through both general and special revelation, God has never stopped working in history to give human beings the ability to follow him and live just and holy lives.

These biblical selections, however, also point to the ever-present and cyclical problem of human sinfulness and God's redemptive responses. Understanding this cycle allows us to read even the sharp warning God gives to Solomon about cutting Israel out of the land should they turn from God (1 Kgs 9:6–9) as not being the end of the story. Each and every human being, whether Jew or Gentile, can choose to live correctly. But every human being, both Jew and Gentile, sins. Too often, the Old Testament is read as a story of God's punishments, as if sins are not important or ultimately destructive. The chapter selections point to two even more important realities. The first is that divine punishment and human suffering for sin reflect the seriousness of human free will used for sinful and evil purposes. The second is the reality of God's persistence in bringing forgiveness and redemption to people who constantly turn away from him. The story of God's loving desires and actions to transform our rebellious lives should always be the center of our reading of the Old Testament. As we will see for the rest of the book, God himself becomes the human being Jesus so that he can bring healing and redemption in a way much deeper than anything seen in the Old Testament.

Study and Reflection Questions

1. Which parts of the history of the Jewish people were new to you? How do they affect your general understanding of how God interacts with people?

2. Despite love not being mentioned frequently in these texts, what elements of the story point to either God's love of people or the need for people to respond in love to God?

3. Which aspects of the selections instruct modern readers about ways to living morally and self-sacrificially?

$$5$$

Matthew's Gospel of Jesus

Preview

The word "Gospel" means "good news." There are four Gospels in the New Testament, telling the life story of Jesus. They describe his ministry and teachings, and they all culminate in Jesus' trial, death, and **resurrection**. The first thing to note is that the Gospels do not all just tell the story of Jesus with all the same details and from all the same perspectives. There are unique elements in each of the Gospels as well as different emphases. Furthermore, the Catholic understanding of the Holy Spirit's work of biblical inspiration does not include dictating what the writers could write. The authors wrote with the assistance of the Holy Spirit and with their own abilities. They each convey their own understandings of the central importance of Jesus' life, death, and resurrection for the salvation of all people.

The most important element to keep in mind when reading the Gospels is the church's confession about the identity and nature of Jesus. Jesus is the eternal Son of God, who is also called the Word (by John), come as a human. As noted in this book's first chapter, God's taking on a human nature (while keeping his divine nature) is called the **Incarnation**. For this reason, Christians *sometimes avoid saying* that "Jesus came down from heaven and became man." The problem with that statement is that it seems to imply that a human being named Jesus existed in heaven and then came to earth. Rather, Christians often are clearer when they say something like: "The Son (or the Word) took on human nature and became Jesus." This makes it clear that the eternal Son only started existing specifically as Jesus when God the Son became Incarnate in Mary's womb. The Son became human as Jesus only about 2,000 years ago.

We can take a moment and reflect on Christianity's dramatic message when it comes to the Incarnation as it ties to the belief in the **Trinity** outlined in this book's Introduction. Christianity proclaims the truth that the One God is the Father, Son, and Holy Spirit. That the Son became incarnate through Mary means that one Person of the Trinity, a Person who is fully God himself, became Jesus. This happened because the Father, Son, and Holy Spirit willed it. Most specifically, the Incarnation of the Son happened in order to heal us, bodies and souls, through God's own death and resurrection. Many people do not quite understand that Christianity makes such a revolutionary claim. As discussed earlier in the Introduction, part of the reason many people miss such a remarkable teaching comes from the mistaken belief that Jesus is more like God's emissary or devoted follower, rather than being God himself. When reading the Gospels in conjunction with this chapter and the next, consider the fact that they are presenting God living on the earth. God, the Creator of all things, has come to live and die for his own creatures. God joined himself to our human nature such that if we had lived during the time that Jesus walked the earth and taught, we would be watching and listening to God himself walking and talking in his human nature.

In this chapter and the next, we will see how the Gospels of Matthew and John present humanity's amazing and surprising encounter with God the Son. Several additional elements should be kept in mind while reading the stories of God's ministry to humanity, including his arrest and crucifixion. First, the Gospels should be read in light of their Jewish context. The Old Testament witnesses to the special work God started among humanity in anticipation and preparation for his own coming. Jesus himself points to the way that the Old Testament prophesizes about him (Luke 24:27). Second, and with this Jewish context in mind, the

Gospels identify Jesus as the culmination and climax of God's special relationship with the Jewish people. God promised to redeem his people, and he came to redeem his people in a way far more intimate and extraordinary than expected.

Third, the Gospels also are clear that God's work of redemption does not stop among the Jews. This point will become clearer and clearer over the course of this and the following chapters. As Jesus, God initiates a **covenant** of healing and salvation for all human beings. Unlike the Jews who were intended to live apart from **Gentiles** and as witnesses to God in the world ("a light to the nations," as declared in Isa 49:6), the earliest Christians were commanded by Jesus to go out into the world. By introducing the Gospel to the world and baptizing all those who wanted to join the church (the community of disciples), Christians were directed by God to offer all human beings a relationship with God through life in the church. Though this is different from what God commanded the Jews with the Torah, the flow of God's interaction with humanity is clear. Looking backwards, we can see continuity with God's promise to Abraham. God the Son (as Jesus) brings to fulfillment the Father, Son, and Holy Spirit's promise to Abraham that the Jews would be a blessing to all nations. Just as the Jews worshipped God with little direction and instruction prior to Moses, so too the Gentiles could know and worship God to a certain degree before Jesus. Related to this, the very general care for Gentiles, which the book of Jonah reports, also becomes more real and permanent. But, it is through God's special revelation in the Incarnation that both Jews and Gentiles finally come to know life through the healing and transformative presence of God himself.

Questions to Consider while Reading

1. What aspects of Jesus' life and ministry are familiar to you and which are surprising?

2. Imagine reading about Jesus' life in the Gospel of Matthew without any knowledge of Christian teachings. What

elements of the Gospel stand out as most important to the writing?

3. What aspects of the Gospel stand out as presenting God in ways similar to, and different from, those we have seen in our prior biblical readings?

Now Read: Matthew's Gospel

Jesus as Culmination of the Covenant with the Jews

Matthew's Gospel begins with the Son's human birth and lineage: "The book of the genealogy of Jesus Christ, the son of David, the son of Abraham" (Matt 1:1). These two phrases connect Jesus to King David and to Abraham, allowing us to take a closer look at the connection between God's work with the Jews and the fulfillment of that work with Jesus. Specifically, these phrases identify Jesus directly as the inheritor of the covenant as a Jew (i.e. through Abraham) and to the kingship of Israel (i.e. through David). In the Old Testament, David's special relationship with God led to the promise that David's line would persist and remain with God's favor. God spoke through the prophet Nathan to say the following to David:

> I will be a father to him, and he shall be a son to me. If he does wrong, I will reprove him with a human rod and with human punishments; but I will not withdraw my favor from him as I withdrew it from Saul who was before you. Your house and your kingdom are firm forever before me; your throne shall be firmly established forever. (2 Sam 7:14–16)

It is easy to think of Jesus, like any other descendent of a king, as a lucky inheritor of a great honor. But Christians understand that it is the Father, Son, and Holy Spirit who made this promise. God made this promise fully intending that God the Son would be bringing ultimate fulfillment to this promise of blessing and permanence by the **Incarnation**. It is in this same section of the

Bible that David speaks about the permanent covenant God has made with the Jewish people through Abraham: "You have established for yourself your people Israel as your people forever . . . " (2 Sam 7:24). Matthew's simple opening verse proclaims God to have permanently joined himself to the human lines of both Abraham (i.e. the Jewish people) and, even more specifically, David (i.e. the kingly line). Consider Christianity's claim: God made these promises with the perfect knowledge that both the Jews and the throne of David would be secured by his own personal connection to both through his Incarnation.

There is another important relationship Matthew emphasizes throughout his Gospel. It is that between Jesus and Moses. Recall the central place Moses has in Judaism. He was the instrument of the **Exodus** and the receiver of the **Torah**, the Law given by God by which the Jews would live in obedience to God and offer genuine worship. Matthew presents Jesus as a kind of new Moses, while simultaneously presenting Jesus as exceeding Moses in terms of personal authority and power. Like Moses needing to be saved as a baby from a murderous king, eventually needing to leave Egypt to fulfill God's plan for him, and ultimately leading the people with divinely authoritative teachings, these factors are mirrored in Jesus' story. Matthew's Gospel thus unfolds a story of Jesus coming to a role of authority and power which is sacred from the start, but which takes time to come to fruition. Most importantly, Matthew's presentation of Jesus as the new Moses always indicates a superiority of Jesus over Moses. Despite Moses' greatness, he is a faithful creature of God. Jesus is presented as a kind of new Moses, but different. Personally, Jesus is God himself and not a creature, and he brings new and ultimate meaning to the Mosaic dimensions of **salvation history**.

Matthew's Gospel, like the other Gospels, identifies Jesus as the unique Son of God. In the first half of Matthew's Gospel, the title "Son of God" is used, but by the devil (4:3, 6) and demons (8:29). It seems that the evil spirits more easily recognize Jesus' true identity. Nevertheless, Jesus' disciples and his opponents understand Jesus to be different, and in some sense unique. A fair reading of the Gospels does not leave the impression of Jesus as simply a misunderstood moral teacher. This is the later reinterpretation many have tried to give of Jesus. While morality remains central to Jesus' teaching, he also presents himself as uniquely important in a way entirely different from any other moral teacher. Jesus makes it clear that he is equal to the Father and the only source of salvation for human beings. The Christian teaching about the Incarnation ultimately makes sense only in light of Christianity's teaching about God's love. God creates out of love and becomes the Jewish man Jesus in order to bring us healing through his death and resurrection, a healing unachievable through moral lessons of the Old Testament alone. This is because moral lessons can tell us what we *ought* to do, but our human nature wounded by sin will continue to entice us into failing to love God and neighbor as we should.

Jesus' Ministry of Teaching and Healing

Jesus teaches in a variety of ways in Matthew's Gospel. For example, Jesus taught frequently through parables. These are moral and theological lessons told through a simple story. One such is the following from Matt 21:28–30 in which Jesus is teaching to a crowd of people:

> "What is your opinion? A man had two sons. He came to the first and said, 'Son, go out and work in the vineyard today.' He said in reply, 'I will not,' but afterwards he changed his mind and went. The man came to the other son and gave the same order. He said in reply, 'Yes, sir,' but did not go. Which of the two did his father's will?" They answered, "The first." Jesus said to them, "Amen, I say to you, tax collectors and prostitutes are entering the kingdom of God before you."

The power of a parable is found in two elements. First, it is not limited to having just one moral lesson. Second, we perceive different moral lessons depending on where we are in life. In this parable, for example, we can note that neither son acted perfectly, since even the son who actually worked rejected his father's needs at the beginning. We can also note that this same son did eventually do the thing his father needed. Furthermore, Jesus emphasized the idea that understanding those basic parameters of the parable is not good enough. By pointing to tax collectors and prostitutes as those who entered the Kingdom first, he is pointing to the universality of sin. It is not moral perfection which brings us admission to the Kingdom, since all are sinners. It is God's healing love which can make tax collectors, prostitutes, and even the rest of us fit for everlasting life with God and each other.

Matthew's Gospel also includes the famous Sermon on the Mount in chapters 5–7. This section contains a variety of teachings. One element which stands out in the Sermon on the Mount is Jesus' authority. Recall the role of Moses, going up a mountain and receiving the teachings of the Torah. As described in prior chapters, the Torah provides God's commandments by which the Jews live their individual and communal lives. The Jewish and Christian traditions honor Moses as the receiver of God's teachings, not their author. Nevertheless, notice how Jesus teaches during the Sermon on the Mount: "You have heard that it was said, 'You shall not commit adultery.' But I say to you, everyone who looks at a woman with lust has already committed adultery with her in his heart" (Matt 5:27–28). Jesus repeats the moral instruction of the Torah itself as found in Exod 20:14 and then claims an authority to deepen it. That is a claim of authority which makes it clear that his authority is the very authority of God himself. These important moral teachings push us to understand what God's holiness is like and what ours should be like. When we try to live out the radical holiness of Jesus' teachings, it results in our recognition of our failures and sins. This recognition points directly to God's message throughout the Old and New Testaments: God alone can heal us, and God offers this because of his love for us.

The love which Jesus offers to us in his ministry is two-fold, matching the fact that we are wounded in both our spiritual as well as our physical aspects. Matthew 9 provides a pivotal scene, giving us a glimpse of this two-fold aspect of Jesus' ministry. Here we see Jesus' work of healing in both soul and body on full display. Friends of a paralytic have brought the crippled man to Jesus. The obvious healing this man needs is a physical one. But the healing our corrupted souls need is even more important, and for this reason, Jesus says to the man: "Courage, child, your sins are forgiven" (Matt 9:2). This statement scandalizes those present since, of course, they recognize that only God can forgive sins. Jesus immediately knew the hostility directed at him, but he proceeded to bring the healing to completion by telling the man: "Rise, pick up your stretcher, and go home" (Matt 9:6). This short section showcases God's intentions for us, which he achieves through the Incarnation. God wants to heal us, souls and bodies. This major work of total healing is completed only through Jesus' death and resurrection.

Jesus' Death and the Temple

In the last chapter, the Temple's importance to Jewish life was highlighted, because God's presence resided there in a special way. Most importantly, the **Temple** served as a place by and through which the Jewish people could acknowledge their sins and gain forgiveness. Though they had the **Torah** to live by, human nature wounded by original sin prevents every human being from claiming freedom from sin. As described in Chapter 2, original sin refers to the wounded state of humanity which inevitably leads us at times to consciously and voluntarily choose to sin. No amount of moral teaching, whether it is the Torah or the words of Jesus, can remedy this corruption to our nature, which was brought upon us by the sin of Adam and Eve. This condition was a central reason for the Temple. It provided a way for a repentant Jew to acknowledge his sin, apologize for his sin, and make an atoning sacrifice for his sin through the blood of an animal. Recall that God had told Adam and Eve that they would die if they chose to eat from the forbidden tree (Gen 2:16–17). This was not some arbitrary punishment. In fact, we can think of it as the logical result of turning from God, our Creator and constant source of life. Sin is, by definition, a turning away from dependency on God. It is a rejection of loyalty to God and loyalty to acting in a way consistent with God's holy and perfectly good nature. Since Christianity teaches that God himself is our source of life, then turning away from God by sinning necessarily includes us saying "no" to our source of life. In other words, when we choose to sin, we choose to say "no" to the life God provides. That is the same thing as us choosing to say "yes" to death itself.

God the Son's ministry of love and reconciliation was a path destined to travel through the depths of human sin. Jesus was well aware of this and gave multiple warnings. His first prediction of his Passion ("**Passion**" referring to the trial, suffering, and murder of Jesus) is found in Matt 16:21: "From that time on, Jesus began to show his disciples that he must go to Jerusalem and suffer greatly from the elders, the chief priests, and the scribes, and be killed and on the third day be raised." Because Peter neither fully understood the true identity of Jesus nor the fact that Jesus' death and resurrection was needed to bring ultimate healing to humanity, he objected. Jesus responded by saying, "You are an obstacle to me. You are thinking not as God does, but as human beings do" (Matt 16:23). This sounds like a harsh word to a loyal disciple, but the value for readers is in the clarity about Jesus' understanding of his mission. Jesus had brought *in himself* the evidence of God's will for humanity. Again and again, he had healed people spiritually and physically. Again and again, he had taught the people the ways of God. But this ministry was never meant to be limited to those actions, since such a ministry is geared only for preparing us for the possibility of true healing. True healing of humanity marked by the wound of original sin could only be accomplished through the Cross and resurrection.

The relationship between Jesus and the Temple was noted in the last chapter. During his trial, witnesses testified that Jesus had said, "I can destroy the Temple of God and within three days rebuild it" (Matt 26:61). Although Matthew's Gospel does not relate when Jesus actually said this, a very similar statement is recorded in John's Gospel. There, Jesus is recorded as saying, "Destroy this Temple and in three days I will raise it up" (John 2:19). John goes on to explain, "But he was speaking about the Temple of his body"

(John 2:21). The point is that Jesus identifies himself as the new and more important Temple. Indeed, Jesus had even pointed out in his earlier teaching, "I say to you, something greater than the Temple is here" (Matt 12:6). We must keep in mind that Matthew is presenting Jesus as God. Matthew's next step was to show that God had established the Temple in Jerusalem with its sacrificial system to act as a **type** for the true Temple and sacrifice, which would be God incarnate himself. Through the Incarnation, God could be the Temple, and the priest, and the sacrifice. Lastly, God's sacrifice and resurrection would be the thing that destroyed death itself. All of these ideas confirm for Christian readers the idea that God became Jesus so that all of humanity would find in him the place to meet God.

Conclusion

The resurrection of Jesus concludes Matthew's Gospel as it does the others, but lengthy explanations about the resurrection and the effects on humanity are not given. The Gospel authors were living the faith of Christian disciples, including frequent participation in the Eucharist (also called the "Lord's Supper" or "Communion"). Their reason for writing the Gospels was to give an account of God's coming to the world through the Incarnation. At the end of Matthew's Gospel, there is the scene called the "Commissioning of the Disciples" (or alternatively called the "Great Commission"). Jesus appears to the apostles and states,

> All power in heaven and on earth has been given to me. Go, therefore, and make disciples of all nations, baptizing them in the name of the Father, and of the Son, and of the holy Spirit, teaching them to observe all that I have commanded you. And behold, I am with you always, until the end of the age. (Matt 28:18–20)

With these words, the Gospel's purpose shines through in two aspects. The first aspect includes Jesus' direction to the church to seek out and welcome all into a healed relationship with God. Such a relationship begins with baptism into the life of the Trinity.

The second aspect of Jesus' words in the Great Commission includes the directive to teach and observe all that Jesus commanded. Jesus taught about many topics and many things. As seen in Matthew, he taught in parables as well as in more direct ways, such as in the Sermon on the Mount. All the details of these teachings are important because they all point to God's holiness and goodness. They also point to God's demand that we strive to live out lives of love and holiness fueled by God's love for us. That love entails God's own suffering and death to bring us healing. Furthermore, Jesus himself gives a kind of shorthand for thinking about the many responsibilities that disciples take on when they join the church. Only in the light of God's own love for us which brought him to his death can we begin to understand his teaching in which he said: "You shall love the Lord, your God, with all your heart, with all your soul, and with all your mind. This is the greatest and the first commandment. The second is like it: You shall love your neighbor as yourself. The whole law and the prophets depend on these two commandments" (Matt 22:37–40).

Study and Reflection Questions

1. What teaching by Jesus stood out to you in a powerful way?

2. Aside from specific teachings (like parables or the Sermon on the Mount), what actions by Jesus helped you to understanding the purpose of Matthew's Gospel?

3. What are a few specific examples of the ways Matthew's Gospel teach us about God's love for us and the response we should give that love?

6

John's Gospel of Jesus

Preview

John's Gospel begins with a radical revelation which reorients Genesis 1. Recall Genesis's imagery of God speaking creation into being. Genesis 1:3 states: "And God said: Let there be light, and there was light." Playing off this portrayal of God in human terms (with God speaking as if he was a human being), John's Gospel begins: "In the beginning was the Word, and the Word was with God, and the Word was God" (John 1:1). John has dramatically adapted Genesis's depiction of God speaking. He has replaced the activity of God speaking in Genesis with a Person whom John identifies here simply as "the Word." Shortly after, John identifies this Person who is the Word as Jesus. In addition to being the Word who is both with God and is God, John 1 identifies the Word as the Creator, the Light of the world, the source of all grace, and as the Person who empowers all people to become children of God. The identity of this Person whom John calls the Word is clear. The Word is Jesus (John 1:17). John 1:14 says: "And the Word became flesh and made his dwelling among us, and we saw his glory, the glory as of the Father's only Son, full of grace and truth." As noted, John teaches that there is one Person being referred to with this variety of names. The eternal Son/Word, who is a divine Person, took on human nature and thus became known from that time on as Jesus. Most important for our understanding, this divine Person (the Word/Son/Jesus) is distinct from the divine Person who is God the Father.

The clarity of John's identification of Jesus as truly God is central to the Gospel. Although this same teaching is just as significant in Matthew's Gospel, differences between the presentations of Jesus' life and ministry are important. For example, John's clarity about the role of the Word/Son with the Father in creating is not presented by Matthew. Matthew introduces the theme of Jesus' divine identity in different, but powerful, ways. He emphasizes the shock among the Jews when Jesus forgave the sins of the crippled man. He also emphasized Jesus' divine authority by recounting Jesus' use of "but I say" when giving the Sermon on the Mount and deepening Moses' teachings of the Torah. In comparison to Matthew, two elements in John's Gospel stand out as distinct. First, John offers a uniquely strong theological perspective throughout his Gospel, explaining clearly to the reader who Jesus is and why he came. Second, John recounts Jesus as speaking far more directly about his identity and the purpose of his ministry than what the other three Gospels present.

One well-known example of John's theological perspective was already discussed in the Introduction. There the example of John 3:16 was given to demonstrate how the term "God" is often used in the Scriptures to designate the Person who is God the Father. Recall John 3:16: "For God so loved the world that he gave his only Son, so that everyone who believes in him might not perish but might have eternal life." Without John 1:1, we might be tempted to think that this reference to "God" in 3:16 excluded the possibility that the Son is also divine. But John 1:1 clearly asserts the Son's divinity: "In the beginning was the Word, and the Word was with God, and the Word was God." When we combine these elements of John's theological perspective with those found throughout the Gospel, the meaning becomes clear. John is saying: God the Father loved the world and gave God the Son in the **Incarnation** for the world's salvation. This is a simplified statement to which many other concepts must be applied to really understand the depths of John's thinking. For example, Jesus himself speaks about the Holy Spirit and the role this third divine Person also plays. Furthermore, we can point to the unity of the Persons in terms of the ability to see that the Father, Son, and Holy Spirit act in perfect unity and harmony. Jesus, in other words, loves the world like the Father and is "sent" in that the Son alone becomes Incarnate. Keeping this web of ideas in mind helps us to appreciate the power and complexity of John's Gospel as John attempts to articulate the experience of meeting God in Jesus, while knowing the distinction of the Father and Holy Spirit from the Son.

When it comes to Jesus' own understanding of himself, one element to notice is the number of times Jesus refers to himself as "I AM." Many biblical translations, including the NABRE, use full capitalization in several places. This is because there are Old Testament examples of this same phrasing being used for **Yahweh** (this being the name for the God of Israel). In other words, Jesus identifies himself with Jewish language only applicable to the one Lord God. One such example can be found in John 8. When challenged by scribes and Pharisees about his authority, Jesus suggested that even Abraham was subservient to him. When further challenged, Jesus said, "Amen, amen, I say to you, before Abraham came to be, I AM" (John 8:58). In this Jewish context, his opponents immediately recognized that Jesus was not only elevating himself above Abraham, but he even was going so far as to make himself equal to God. Their response to this was, unsurprisingly, violence: "So they picked up stones to throw at him; but Jesus hid and went out of the Temple area" (John 8:59). When reading John's Gospel, pay close attention to the power and the clarity in Jesus' expression of himself as Son of God.

Questions to Consider while Reading

1. Aside from those examples given in this chapter's Preview section, what other element can you find in John's Gospel which points to Jesus' divine identity?

2. Can you identify a teaching of Jesus which is not explicitly talking about "love," but which really cannot be understood apart from the idea that God loves us and wants to heal us?

3. What are a few elements in John's Gospel which help to deepen your understanding of God?

Now Read: John's Gospel

Judgment in John's Gospel

John's Gospel sometimes presents Jesus talking about other people in quite harsh or uncompromising terms. We see this at times in the way that Jesus teaches and acts. We also see it in the commentary which the author of the Gospel threads through it. Before commenting further on this, it is helpful to point out that this is not unique to John. Recall in Matthew's Gospel some of Jesus' harsher teachings in chapter 23. One such teaching was the following:

> Woe to you, scribes and Pharisees, you hypocrites. You are like whitewashed tombs, which appear beautiful on the outside, but inside are full of dead men's bones and every kind of filth. Even so, on the outside you appear righteous, but inside you are filled with hypocrisy and evildoing. (Matt 23:27–28)

Though many people find harsh and condemnatory words offensive, it is likely that more than a few readers encountered this aspect of Jesus for the first time when reading Matthew's Gospel along with the prior chapter of this book. Jesus is often believed to be too nice to judge. He is often thought of as too caring to speak harshly. He is likewise often thought of as too meek to challenge us. But here again, this is not the Jesus of the Gospels. Because God loves us, he will always challenge the sin and evil in our lives which brings about our corruption and death.

Despite the basic understanding of Jesus as very mild, many people often still know about the story of Jesus cleansing the **Temple** in Jerusalem. It is told in all four of the Gospels. However, in the Synoptic Gospels (Matthew, Mark, and Luke), this episode coincides with Jesus' entry into Jerusalem just before his arrest and trial. Matthew's Gospel states: "Jesus entered the Temple area and drove out all those engaged in selling and buying there" (Matt 21:12). Many read this section as a relatively spontaneous action. Jesus went to the Temple and encountered corruption. It angered him, and he started flipping the tables over. He could not stand the disrespect to God's house. Such passionate anger is understandable to everyone. Such a response does not really challenge the view many have of Jesus as mild because we have all lost our tempers. In the Synoptic Gospels, the physical challenge to the religious authorities is followed soon after by Jesus' arrest and execution The religious authorities did not find Jesus mild, but rather threatening.

There are important details about the event of the cleansing of the Temple which are different in John's Gospel. First, the cleansing of the Temple happens at the beginning of Jesus' ministry in John. The episode occurs just after Jesus' first miracle, when Jesus turned water into wine at the Cana wedding (John 2). After the wedding, Jesus, along with his mother, brothers, and disciples head to Jerusalem where this event happens. Therefore, a very direct physical encounter is presented by John as part of the beginning of Jesus' ministry. Such a factor helps to explain the anger and hostility directed at Jesus from the various religious authorities. But the second element is perhaps even more important, for John's Gospel states: "He made a whip out of cords and drove them all out of the Temple area" (John 2:15). This whip-making took at least a little time. It took intentionality. John therefore presents the cleansing of the Temple as God's direct challenge to the pollution there. In John's telling, we are not really given the option of interpreting the story as we might with the other Gospels in which Jesus may have acted spontaneously and with little thought. The Temple's sanctity was being trampled upon. Jesus acted out of a righteous anger, and righteous anger has the object of correcting sin and allowing the recipient of that anger to reconsider the sin in his life. God's anger and judgment are ultimately meant to restore human beings who repent of their sins and seek to change their ways.

The anger God has about sin and his judgment of it warn us about the consequences we can expect when we choose sin. In John's Gospel, this point is connected to the themes of light and dark. After describing God's love for the world and God's willingness to be sacrificed and die for the world because of this love, John 3 goes on to say:

> And this is the verdict, that the light came into the world, but people preferred darkness to light, because their works were evil. For everyone who does wicked things hates the light and does not come toward the light, so that his works might not be exposed. But whoever lives the truth comes to the light, so that his works may be clearly seen as done in God. (John 3:19–21)

John is not suggesting that there are perfectly righteous human beings and perfectly evil ones. The Gospel makes it clear that God comes to minister to all those willing to receive it. He also came to die for all human beings because all human beings are sinners. Those who wish to be healed of their sins by God are identified as loving the light. But there are still those who prefer their sins and reject the healing and righteousness only God can give. In John's Gospel, they are said to prefer the darkness and all of the consequences which come. This is strong language indeed, and it is clearly a central feature of John's work.

The Eucharist

"Eucharist" comes from the Greek word meaning "thanksgiving." Since the early days of the church, it has been used to refer to the sacrament which is also called the "Lord's Supper" or "Communion." The word "sacrament" refers to a specific sacred ritual which brings members of the church into direct contact with God and God's graces. Jesus commanded his disciples to share in his presence through this ritual using bread and wine for his body and blood. Matthew, Mark, and Luke, as well as Paul in his First Letter to the Corinthians, all describe the event in which Jesus gave his disciples the command and instructions for this sacred ritual. The use of the Greek word "Eucharist" comes from the fact that when Jesus established the ritual, he "gave thanks" over the bread and wine (Matt 26:27, Mark 14:23, Luke 21:17, 1 Cor 11:24). Although there are today a few different ways that Christians understand the Eucharist, the central importance of this sacrament has been a part of the life of the church since its beginning.

Curiously, the Last Supper account in John 13–17 does not include an institution of the Eucharist as can be found in the other Gospels. Instead, John's Gospel contains an extended scene in chapter 6 of a miraculous feeding and then a teaching called "The Bread of Life Discourse." The Catholic Church points to this episode as Jesus giving his first message of what would be his later institution of the Eucharist. Jesus in this section teaches that he himself is the bread of life. John 6 reports:

> So Jesus said to them, "Amen, amen, I say to you, it was not Moses who gave the bread from heaven; my Father gives you the true bread from heaven. For the bread of God is that which comes down from heaven and gives life to the world." So they said to him, "Sir, give us this bread always." Jesus said to them, "I am the bread of life; whoever comes to me will never hunger, and whoever believes in me will never thirst." (John 6:32–35)

It would be easy to spiritualize or symbolize this teaching, but many of Jesus' listeners take offence at these comments and challenge him for saying that he was the bread from heaven. In response, Jesus replied, "I am the living bread that came down from heaven; whoever eats this bread will live forever; and the bread that I will give is my flesh for the life of the world" (John 6:51). Jesus does not just challenge the indignation some had about his claim to such significance; he emphasizes a literalism about his words.

When confronted more directly by the seriousness of calling himself food to be eaten, some of those talking with Jesus responded, "How can this man give us [his] flesh to eat?" (John

6:52). Clearly, these people thought that Jesus was suggesting cannibalism, and they were repulsed by it. Nevertheless, Jesus' teaching continues in a graphic way. He responds by saying, "Amen, amen, I say to you, unless you eat the flesh of the Son of Man and drink his blood, you do not have life within you. Whoever eats my flesh and drinks my blood has eternal life, and I will raise him on the last day. For my flesh is true food, and my blood is true drink" (John 6:54–56). Jesus can be seen here as challenging those who followed him. He is telling them words that do not yet make sense, since he has not yet revealed the sacramental nature of the Eucharist. Despite this, Jesus' disciples had plenty of the reasons to continue to trust and follow him, but some did not: "As a result of this, many [of] his disciples returned to their former way of life and no longer accompanied him" (John 6:66). Such disciples were willing to follow Jesus only on their own terms and with their own understanding. They were unwilling to conform their ideas to the greater truths which God was there revealing to them.

John's Gospel was written in a community perhaps more than sixty years after Jesus' **resurrection**. These were Christians who lived their faith through the light of the Eucharist. But John chose to present this announcement of the Eucharist as a way of demonstrating the different responses to Jesus. As noted above, the themes of light and dark throughout the Gospel indicate whether people are abandoning their sin by trusting in God to live in the light or choosing to remain in the darkness. Those who were confronted by Jesus' words about the Eucharist, words which point to the need for all human beings to be transformed body and soul by contact with Jesus, had to make a choice. Many of those who were disciples because they had heard Jesus' teachings and seen his miracles abandoned him because of their confusion and lack of trust. The apostles, however, did not. When asked by Jesus whether they too would turn their backs on him, Peter responded by saying: "Master, to whom shall we go? You have the words of eternal life" (John 6:68). Although it seems counterintuitive, John's Gospel presents a relatively common phenomenon: despite seeing and hearing what is recognizable as God's love and desire to heal us, many people seem to turn away from accepting those things for one reason or another.

God's Love and the Obedience of Disciples

The themes of light and darkness, mercy and judgment, and belief and unbelief are presented by John first and foremost through the lens of God's love. As we saw in John 3:16, it is God's love that comes first. God created out of love. Although humanity is imperiled by its sinful rebellion, God continues to love: "For God so loved the world that he gave his only Son, so that everyone who believes in him might not perish but might have eternal life" (John 3:16). This message of God loving his creation, and most especially the human beings of his creation, is consistent throughout the entire Christian Bible, the Old Testament and New Testament alike. But the love which God offers is not a love of acceptance for all that human beings are and do. Today, we often hear about unconditional love as if it begins and ends in a celebration of all aspects about us. This is not the unconditional love of God, just as the unconditional love a mother has for her child does not include celebrating or encouraging self-destructive behaviors. God's unconditional love is the radical love of our Creator who himself heals us of our weaknesses and sins so that we can live healed lives. God does not accept our brokenness and our rebellion in sin as a good thing. Instead, God offers us a life of health and fullness when we decide to follow his will. Following his will means living and loving as he does.

The best example and model of love is that which is seen between the Persons of the **Trinity**. The Father loves the Son, and the Son loves the Father. This is an element central to John's Gospel. Jesus states, "As the Father loves me, so I also love you. Remain in my love" (John 15:9). We will explore some other main ideas in John 15, but reflecting on verse 9 for a moment can help us understand the rest. Jesus proclaims that his relationship with the Father is based upon love. This verse comes not long after Jesus proclaims his own love for the Father: " . . . but the world must know that I love the Father and that I do just as the Father has commanded me" (John 14:31). As we will see in our work in chapter 8, these ideas reflect the similar assertion in 1 John 4:8 that "whoever is without love does not know God, for God is love." The straightforward assertion that "God is love" uniquely expresses the heart of Christianity. God is revealed as a Trinity of Persons who love each other. That is the nature of the one God of Christianity. God actually loves eternally, because the Father, Son, and Holy Spirit love each other eternally and, therefore, before creation. God did not begin to finally love when God created. God created in order to share with us the perfect love already expressed between the Father, Son, and Holy Spirit.

The central role of obedience is the other major element of John 15's presentation of God's love. When the Son becomes Incarnate as Jesus, he gives us a chance to see perfect obedience. Jesus talks about his love for the Father and gives us his human example of obedience. As noted above, Christianity teaches that God loves us unconditionally. However, God's unconditional love never leaves the willing human being in a state of sin and rebellion. God never says, "You are good enough." Rather, God teaches us that we can live in abundance based on the healing he gives through loving and obeying him. After Jesus tells us of the Father's love for him, he says: "If you keep my commandments, you will remain in my love, just as I have kept my Father's commandments and remain in his love" (John 15:10). Many people today think about obedience as something suitable for children. Yet obedience to living as God teaches is the prerequisite of experiencing the peace and fullness of life which God can and will give us. To try to live righteously in all things as God commands us is not simple. Jesus gives us a radical command which challenges us to see God's presence and expectations in every moment of every day in our lives: "This I command you: love one another" (John 15:17).

Conclusion

When we look back through the topics introduced in this chapter, we can hopefully see a clear relationship between them. The harsh language of judgment and challenge suits God's holy response to human sin and rebellion. Christianity does not look at this beautiful world with all of its many joys and blessings only to ignore the darkness. This world is filled with unspeakable darkness which we can find all around us, as well as in us. God's Incarnation as Jesus is the event which confronts all the evil the world has ever known or will ever know. As Jesus, God has come to conquer it. God does this because of his infinite love for us all. God loves the world and God loves us. God's love for his sinful children is the reason for his willingness to offer himself as a sacrifice on the Cross. The darkness in which we individually and collectively participate is no match for God's power to recreate and restore us in our relationship with him and each other.

Judgment and love thus go hand in hand because we live in a world we corrupt. Had we never sinned, we would never have known the hardships of a world which suffers and causes suffering. We would have remained in God's love and peace and been all the happier for it. But, the world is fallen, as are we. And God loves us infinitely more than we can understand. We are asked to respond to his love and his commands so that we can be healed and share that love. The culmination of that love is experienced through God's unique sacramental presence in the Eucharist. God has not only taught us, healed us, and walked with us spiritually. God is there in the Eucharist entirely, both physically and spiritually. Catholicism speaks about the Eucharist as the pinnacle of faith because each time one experiences it, one experiences Jesus Christ completely and personally. Jesus' Bread of Life Discourse invites us to trust that God's love conquers all that brings us suffering and ultimately death. Jesus' Bread of Life Discourse invites us to accept being a disciple of Jesus and then obey the Father in all things so that we too can remain in the love of God.

Study and Reflection Questions

1. Apart from examples used in this chapter about such themes as light and darkness, mercy and judgment, or obedience and

disobedience, what details did you see in John which help to explain God's reaction to sin?

2. How can the Bread of Life discourse be seen as God offering his loving healing to his followers even though many turned away? What other elements of John's Gospel can help us make sense of John 6?

3. Can you identify any passages in John and Matthew which help us understand the similarities and differences in the presentations those two Gospels give of Jesus' obedience?

7

The Apostles' Witness to the Word and the World

Preview

This chapter offers a glimpse into the formation and expansion of the church. We will recall that Jesus' commission to the eleven remaining apostles at the end of Matthew's Gospel included the following:

> All power in heaven and on earth has been given to me. Go, therefore, and make disciples of all nations, baptizing them in the name of the Father, and of the Son, and of the holy Spirit, teaching them to observe all that I have commanded you. And behold, I am with you always, until the end of the age. (Matt 28:18–20)

The disciples were commanded to witness to Jesus' teachings and ministry. Furthermore, this witnessing included a trinitarian baptismal formula, since it is done in the name of the Father, Son, and Holy Spirit. Jesus gave his disciples an assurance of his own power to help them fulfill this mission. This power enabled the church to make disciples in all nations by inviting them into the covenantal relationship God offers all human beings through Jesus. At this point, we might recall that the church's power to act as Christ's body after his ascension is always associated with the presence of the Holy Spirit. John 16 reports Jesus' promise that he would send the Spirit to empower and guide the church.

The readings for this chapter include different kinds of texts. With the selections from the Acts of the Apostles, we get narratives about the apostles and the beginning of the church, along with more individual stories about Peter, Paul, and others. The letter to the Galatians and the selection from the letter to the Romans are different types of writings. They are letters, and not quite like the selective history of the early church given in the Acts of the Apostles. Though Paul appears in the Acts of the Apostles as a major figure, it was Luke who wrote both the Gospel and Acts. Paul, however, is the author of both Galatians and Romans. We also must keep in mind that this Paul is the same person known first by the name "Saul" in the Acts of the Apostles. He is the one vigorously persecuting the church. By combining the narratives from the Acts of the Apostles with the more direct instructions to the communities of Galatia and Rome, we will be able to see the ways in which the Scriptures point to the unity of the actions and teachings of the church from different perspectives. Despite the differences between reading sections from a history and reading letters, this chapter's selections all engage the topics of faith, love, and self-sacrifice. These selections also point to the ways in which Jesus established the church in order to continue his ministry of teaching and healing.

A major issue, to which this chapter will return shortly, concerns **Gentile** believers (i.e. those Christians who were not Jewish by birth). Recall the nature of the **covenant** given to Abraham and his descendants. God established a covenant with the Jewish people in order for them to be a "light to the nations" (Isa 49:6). The light refers to the fact that the **chosen people** are to be faithful to God's **Torah**. Jewish fidelity to the Torah in turn points to God's desire to be present to all of his children in all nations. When we studied the book of Jonah, we saw the themes of God's love and concern for Gentiles, even those who were enemies of Israel. This does not conflict with the general requirement of the Torah for Jews to segregate themselves from most aspects of social life with Gentiles. Being a light to the nations does not actually necessitate mixing with, or living in close proximity to, Gentile social practices.

The topics of faith, love, and self-sacrifice in the scriptural selections of this chapter will come to light in terms of the newly-founded church's growing self-understanding. Since God himself came as the Jewish man Jesus in order to fulfill the covenant he had made with the Jews, it was natural for the first disciples to be Jews themselves. That is why the early church is characterized as being composed almost exclusively of Jewish Christians. This term refers to the early church members who were Jewish by birth, but also followers of Jesus the **Messiah**, or the **Christ**. The first disciples understood the way in which God had prepared the Jewish people to understand and receive the Messiah. However, change quickly came to the church's composition because of Christ's commission to the church to go out into the nations and to make believers of all peoples. This is something like the opposite of the restrictions the Torah put on Jews in terms of contact with Gentiles. For this reason, the church began to quickly morph from being Jewish Christian to mainly Gentile Christians. As you read the selections from the Scriptures, notice how the themes of faith, love, and self-sacrifice dominate the concerns of the church's demographic changes.

Questions to Consider while Reading

1. What details stand out to you in the life of the early church which are either new or seen in a different light with this reading of Acts?

2. How would you explain your understanding of the freedom from the Torah yet the requirement to live with obligations to act in certain ways?

3. How is Paul's description of self-sacrificial love similar to, or different from, the prior descriptions of love seen in the scriptural selections chosen for this book?

Now Read: Acts 1–10 and 15; Galatians; and Rom 12–15

Acts of the Apostles and the Holy Spirit

The Acts of the Apostles begins with Jesus' promise of the Holy Spirit (chapter 1) and proceeds to the Spirit's coming to rest upon the disciples. This event in Acts 2 fulfills Jesus' promise and sets the stage for the rest of the stories in Acts. In chapter 2, the result of the Spirit's coming can be described as power and courage given to the disciples. This is a stark change, especially considering the disciples' last major encounter with the religious authorities during Jesus' arrest and murder. During Jesus' **Passion**, Peter showed himself to be a less than ideal disciple. He denied knowing Jesus multiple times. That was before the gift of the Spirit and the knowledge of Jesus' victory over death in the resurrection. Now in Acts, Peter's response to the Spirit's coming on Pentecost leads to him giving a courageous, stunning, and very public first sermon by the church. As shown repeatedly through Acts and the rest of the New Testament, the church would no longer fear persecution.

The power of the Spirit moved many of those who heard Peter's first sermon. This sermon concluded by pointing to Jesus as "both Lord and Messiah, this Jesus whom you [the people of Jerusalem] crucified" (Acts 2:36). The clarity of Jesus' identity was beginning to sink in now that Peter could walk the people through the ways in which Jesus fulfilled the many promises of the Old Testament. It could also sink in because of the clarity, power, and authority by which Peter spoke, since he was a simple fisherman by trade. The people were desperate to make themselves right with God: "Now when they heard this, they were cut to the heart, and they asked Peter, 'What are we to do, my brothers?'" (Acts 2:37). Peter's response seems simple, but it takes into account his hearers' understanding of God's promises to the Jews as well as the Torah itself. Peter states: "Repent and be baptized, every one of you, in the name of Jesus Christ for the forgiveness of your sins; and you will receive the gift of the holy Spirit" (Acts 2:38). According to the book of Acts, 3,000 people became disciples of Jesus that day in response to this evangelization.

Although numerous figures appear in the selections we are reading from Acts, Peter and Paul stand out as the primary figures. Peter and his brother Andrew were the very first disciples whom Jesus called (Matt 4:18–20). They followed without hesitation. We have seen in the Gospels that they were not perfect disciples. Nevertheless, Peter learned to love and trust Jesus as the years went by, and by the time Jesus ascended and left the disciples with the Spirit, Peter was a recognized leader of great love and devotion to the church. This still did not give Peter absolutely perfect judgment. However, it did give him the humility to listen for God's voice, no matter the circumstance or source. His calling to preach to the Gentile leader Cornelius, for example, began the process by which his Jewish identity and his understanding of God's activity in **Christ** began to change. After preaching to Cornelius and his household, Peter witnessed the gift of the Holy Spirit coming upon them. This allowed him to see that God was leading the Christian community to a new relationship with all human beings. He therefore accepted God's leading and proceeded to baptize the Gentiles as full members of the church.

Unlike Peter, Saul (also called Paul) began his relationship with the church as a persecutor. Saul believed that Jesus and his followers were blasphemers who should be punished for insulting God and corrupting Jewish belief. This came from his understanding of the Torah and what he thought his devotion to it required. Acts 9:1 describes Saul as "breathing murderous threats against the disciples of the Lord." Saul's vision of Jesus on his way to arrest disciples in Damascus forced him to reconsider God's activity in the world. As a result of Jesus striking Saul blind and then sending a disciple to heal him, Saul was baptized and immediately began proclaiming that Jesus was the Son of God and the hoped-for **Messiah** of Israel (Acts 9:20–22). This story of Saul's conversion seems to have some relationship to Saul being known by the church as Paul, though Acts 13:9 states that Saul and Paul were both names he used. Like Jesus changing Simon's name to

Peter (Matt 16:18), Paul's transition to becoming a completely devoted servant of Christ may have had something to do with him becoming almost exclusively referred to as Paul in all of our sources after becoming a follower of Jesus.

Galatians and the Transformation of the Church

Paul became a devoted follower of Jesus because he saw Jesus as the fulfillment of God's promises to Israel and the world. Jesus was the long-awaited—but surprising—Messiah, whose death and resurrection brought human redemption. In the book of Galatians, we find Paul responding to a group of people who seem to be teaching the need to follow the **Torah**, or at least parts, in order to be Christian. Historically, these people are known as Judaizers, because it is understood that they were teaching a message that being observant of the Torah, like a faithful Jew, was necessary for salvation. To this, Paul responded: "O stupid Galatians! Who has bewitched you, before whose eyes Jesus Christ was publically portrayed as crucified? I want to learn only this from you: did you receive the Spirit from works of the law, or from faith in what you heard?" (Gal 3:1–2). Of course, Paul's response is that works cannot heal us or make us right with God. Only God can do that for us by dying and rising on our behalf. Jesus' death and resurrection can wrap us all into Jesus' redemption, especially in light of Jesus' emphasis on participation in baptism and the Eucharist. Therefore, despite the rules of the Torah (such as circumcision, eating restrictions, purification rituals, and the sacrifices of the Temple), Jesus revealed that those Laws had one central goal. The Torah was given to human beings to help us realize that God requires our obedience, but that our obedience does not cure our sinfulness; only God can heal us of that.

In Galatians, Paul also records the struggle within the church of coming to clarity about this issue of works (or the Law) and faith. Paul points to his own confrontation with Peter (who is called here in Galatians "Cephas"). Peter had known that the Jewish dietary laws no longer applied to one who had received the Holy Spirit through faith in Jesus' saving work. Peter realized this when he saw the Gentile Cornelius and Cornelius's whole household receive the Holy Spirit after Peter's preaching to them. In Antioch, Peter had begun sharing meals with Gentile Christians because all Christians are equally accepted by God. But other Jewish Christians came and Peter started avoiding mixing with the Gentile Christians. Paul wrote: "But when I saw that they were not on the right road in line with the truth of the gospel, I said to Cephas in front of all, 'If you, though a Jew, are living like a Gentile and not like a Jew, how can you compel the Gentiles to live like Jews?'" (Gal 2:14). Paul's point is that salvation can only come through faith in Jesus and not through obedience to the Torah, called "laws" in Gal 2:16. To make Gentile Christians feel like they are not really Christians for not living like Torah-obedient Jews is to violate the true message of the Gospel. This harms the relationships within the church between Jewish Christians and Gentile Christians.

Paul also reminds the Galatians that his teaching about the centrality of faith comes directly from *Peter's* own experiences, as well as the judgment of the church at the Council of Jerusalem (Acts 15). This is not Paul's own special interpretation. The very life of the church depended on the ability for all of her members to know, preach, and live the same Gospel. For this reason, Paul explains that the Law acted in a way to help the Jews understand the need for humility. Not only could no one fulfill all of the Torah perfectly, but the Torah itself pointed to the fact that only God can, and does, redeem human beings. This is why Paul contrasts living by laws with living by faith. Faith is the ability to say "yes, and thank you" to God for the gift of salvation through Jesus **Christ**. Faith by definition accepts God's grace, or gifts, as the only way we can be made right with God. Paul warns: "You are separated from Christ, you who are trying to be justified by law; you have fallen from grace" (Gal 5:4). Paul clearly understands that Christians have real responsibilities to love and serve God and others, but living out those responsibilities is part of the "thank you" to the God who has already made salvation and healing a reality through his Passion and resurrection.

In Galatians, Paul witnesses to the Gospel which he received from God: God offers salvation and healing to all human beings through his **Incarnation** as Jesus Christ. Freedom from needing to obey some aspects of the Torah, specifically those which separated Jews from living intimately with Gentiles, enabled all to live in the freedom to serve the other members of the church and all human beings. To emphasize these points, Paul writes: "For you were called to freedom, brothers. But do not use this freedom as an opportunity for the flesh; rather, serve one another through love. For the whole law is fulfilled in one statement, namely, 'You shall love your neighbor as yourself'" (Gal 5:13–14). Although we cannot earn our salvation, God transforms us through our faith. Faith in God's work through Jesus brings about transformation by the Spirit. And the presence of the Spirit in the lives of the church members brings about their empowerment to love. Therefore, freedom from the Torah is not freedom from responsibility. Christian freedom is the freedom to be empowered by the Holy Spirit to be self-sacrificially loving like Jesus, and thus perhaps even loving to the point of dying for others.

Romans and Love

When Paul wrote to the Romans, he was not writing to a church which he established. This makes Romans different from the letter to the Galatians. Paul had helped found the Galatian church, and he was writing to correct them of an error which they had embraced in his absence. Paul's letter to the Roman Church is different in that Paul is writing to introduce himself. He is writing to help the Roman Christians see and understand the way he teaches the Gospel in anticipation of his coming to them. The main theme that this section will focus on concerns love. We will see how Paul thinks of love in light of the gifts Christians receive from God, love in light of the responsibility to obey God's commandments, and love in light of the way Christians should live self-sacrificially for others.

Many spiritual people think first and foremost about creation and life when they think about gifts from God. Everything other than God exists because God willed it. From the Christian perspective, another way of saying this is that God loved creation into existence. As we saw in Genesis 1 and especially in John's adaptation of Genesis's themes, God did not need to create. God created because God had a will to share the eternal love experienced between the Father, Son, and Holy Spirit. Christians likewise think about gifts in very specific ways. Paul, for example, points out that specific, individual graces (gifts) should not make us think that we are better than anyone else (Rom 12:3). Paul, here and in 1 Corinthians, uses the image of a body for the ways in which different parts of the body all work together. All the different parts of the body are necessary for a healthy body to function, whether that be the head, feet, or heart. And what those parts do, they do simultaneously for their own good and the good of the whole body. Thus Paul teaches: "Since we have gifts that differ according to the grace given to us, let us exercise them" (Rom 12:6). Each individual Christian has been given specific and unique gifts, but they were not given just for his or her own benefit. Each individual Christian possesses gifts which were, and are, meant to be shared lovingly with the church and with the world.

In prior chapters, we have seen the importance of the Torah's instructions, or laws, including circumcision and the well-known prohibitions against eating pork. However, the **Ten Commandments** are also part of the Torah, as are many other moral laws. Furthermore, Jewish tradition has always taught that every single human being is required to keep the moral laws which can be known by all, like the prohibitions against lying, theft, murder, etc. For both the Jewish and Christian traditions, following such laws are neither thought of as a burden nor as something to do because of feared punishment, since those ideas misunderstand God's commandments entirely. Rather, God's commandments reflect his instructions to us so that we can live full lives. Sins are those actions which depart from God's will for us, and therefore they drive us away from what can bring us true and lasting happiness.

In Paul's letter to the Romans, he reminds the church of the central connection love has to the moral laws:

> The commandments, "You shall not commit adultery; you shall not kill; you shall not steal; you shall not covet," and whatever other commandment there may be, are all summed up in this saying, [namely] "You shall love your neighbor as yourself." Love does no evil to the neighbor; hence, love is the fulfillment of the law. (Rom 13:9–10)

Paul reminds us that real love for God and others produces all of the kinds of actions which God commands for us, since God commands those things which make life good, true, and worth living.

Paul includes the topic of self-denial as part of his teachings about love. As we all know, even in loving communities such as families and churches, human relationships are difficult and complicated. We know that on some occasions we are weak in expressing our love for others or in not putting others before ourselves. Paul teaches the patient nurturing which must govern our lives: "We who are strong ought to put up with the failings of the weak and not to please ourselves; let each of us please our neighbor for the good, for building up" (Rom 15:1–2). Paul in the prior chapter had detailed the scandal some Christians experienced over food. It seems that some believed that certain foods were inappropriate for Christians to eat. Paul's pastoral advice of not trying to please ourselves is a challenge which includes many important elements to consider. The advice Paul gives seems clearly applicable in some circumstances and quite problematic in others. Therefore, it is good to keep the principles of self-denial and self-sacrifice in mind as the focus of Paul's thinking. This leads to the ability of the church to discern how best to live out Paul's advice in different circumstances.

Conclusion

The themes discussed above give us an important picture of the connection between gifts and self-sacrifice. On the one hand,

Christians understand that all the common and all the unique gifts which God has given them are meant to be shared for the benefit of others. On the other hand, we have seen a central tradition in Christianity by which self-sacrifice is understood as necessary for creating loving relationships. There is probably nothing very surprising about these ideas to most people. However, many people, probably many Christians, do not often think about how central these ideas are to the Scriptures and to Christianity's traditional teachings.

Finally, language of graces and gifts points to the foundation of God in our lives and in salvation. For Christians, the responsible use of the gifts which God has given to each of us means sharing those gifts to strengthen others. The gifts come from God, and the ability of a Christian to effectively put these gifts at the service of others happens through the presence of the Spirit. This is a way of seeing that from the moment of our creation, we are all sharers in God's gifts. God endows us with gifts, his presence, and the strength to live as he lives. Such dynamics make us grateful sharers in his life and power. With these factors in mind, we are better able to appreciate the Christian idea of salvation as coming from God and not from ourselves. Another way of putting it is that we participate in God's work of salvation by accepting the renewal which God alone has given us, first with creation and then with his own shared life through the Cross and resurrection.

Study and Reflection Questions

1. What are a few aspects of these readings about the church's early life which seem connected to Jesus' ministry in Matthew and John?

2. From your reading of Galatians, how would you describe Paul's vision of unity within the church between Jewish Christians and Gentile Christians?

3. What kinds of situations have you encountered where you could apply Paul's advice about loving self-sacrifice?

8

The Word of God in the Life of the Church

Preview

The two Scripture readings accompanying this chapter address the reality that human life, even the life in the church, is complicated despite gifts from God, our greatest ideas, and our greatest achievements. It is filled with everyone's good acts and sinful acts. Human life is difficult and confusing. This points us to a feature which we have seen throughout the Old Testament and the New Testament: the human struggle to love God and each other in the way that reflects God's love for us. Hebrews and 1 John both, in their own ways, exhort readers to seek out the greatest expression of human life, which can only be found in communion with God through Jesus **Christ**. They also strongly challenge the ways in which different teachings and behaviors can turn human beings away from this communion.

The circumstances of Hebrews are different from those of 1 John. In the case of Hebrews, most scholars believe that this letter was written because some Jewish Christians were beginning to turn away from their Christian faith. Technically, the word "apostasy" is used to describe the abandonment of a once-held faith. It is most likely that some Jewish Christians were turning away from Christian faith and back to a specifically Jewish expression of faith. The author of Hebrews writes to lay out the reasons for this error and to warn against it. In the case of 1 John, the letter speaks to a different kind of challenge to the faith. The seeming challenge described by this letter is not apostasy but rather heresy. "Heresy," coming from the Greek word which in part means "opinion," refers to a teaching about the faith which contradicts traditional beliefs of the community. The author warns against a certain faction of the church which appears to reject the doctrine of the **Incarnation**. The issue here is not about abandoning the faith for a different one; rather, the issue is about teaching a different version of Christianity in opposition to the teaching of the church. Both Hebrews and 1 John identify these errors and call people to return to the true faith of Christianity in communion with the church.

Today in the West, we live in a highly diverse society. It is filled with people of many different faiths, people who are not sure about faith, those who are not part of an organized religion, and those who are atheists. Most Americans support this diversity specifically because of our political history. Many of our religious traditions are simultaneously becoming more overtly open-minded about other religions. Typically, all of this is seen as a cornerstone of a modern democracy's civil order. We can be sure that even children are taught the outlines of such freedoms when we hear them exclaiming: "It's a free country!" In countries like America, freedom of religious thought and practice are, as a consequence, a major feature of our society. Such concerns are different from, but not contradictory to, Christianity's traditional understanding of the role of faith and the authority of the church. There is a difference between promoting a social order of freedom and recognizing that a religion like Christianity holds that it would be best for all people to embrace Christianity and join the church.

With the above ideas in mind, we can begin by considering what Christians mean when they teach that some beliefs should be accepted and some rejected. To be clear, we are not suggesting simply that different people find different ideas meaningful to them. That is certainly true. People believe plenty of different things. But the issue really is about how we make sense of the fact that Christianity teaches that some beliefs are good and others are bad. Such a stance might sound presumptuous or arrogant, but most people think this way all of the time. We constantly make judgments about what we think helps or harms life, even if we do not try to use the government to stop people from making bad decisions for themselves. In the case of Hebrews and 1 John, we want to investigate the claims about why specific ideas are seen as harmful to people and the church community.

Questions to Consider while Reading

1. Can a teaching which opposes a community's faith be problematic or even dangerous in any way? If so, how?

2. What details about faith stand out to you when reading the texts?

3. What teachings about the importance of Jesus stand out to you in these two texts?

Now Read: Hebrews and 1 John

Hebrews and the Uniqueness of Jesus

In the New Testament sections already studied, every author has found a way to speak about Jesus' uniqueness and his supremacy. For example, in both Matthew and John, we saw the use of "Son of God" language as pointing to Jesus' unique relationship with the Father. We also saw instances of the Son acting and speaking in ways which indicated his equality with the Father. The readings from Acts, Galatians, and Romans also gave various kinds of testimony to a new order of human communion with God through the perfectly united activity of the Father, Son, and Holy Spirit. The Letter to the Hebrews picks up on several of the themes we have already explored and emphasizes them with numerous citations from the Old Testament. As described in the preview above, the author seems concerned with Jewish Christians departing from Christian beliefs and returning to Jewish practice. For this reason, the author goes to greater lengths than others we have seen to demonstrate that Jesus is the fulfillment and the climax of the Jewish tradition. The decision to turn away from Christian belief is being compared by the author with intentionally turning away from having the best possible relationship with God.

The author of Hebrews sticks with themes familiar to an audience steeped in Judaism, though the letter begins with an added universal scope. The author starts by placing the Son at the head of all creation: "In times past, God spoke in partial and various ways to our ancestors through the prophets; in these last days, he spoke to us through a son, whom he made heir of all things and through whom he created the universe" (Heb 1:1–2). Hebrews places Jesus at the head of all creation, because he is being identified as the Creator. In prior chapters, we encountered the struggle the early Christian tradition had in articulating the Son's equality with the Father. This was because the Jewish tradition understood God to be one Person, namely the Father. Here the text tries to express the idea that the Father (called here "God") and the Son both stand above creation. Immediately, Hebrews moves on to compare Jesus to the angels, who had always been seen as having a superior place in the created order. Jesus stands above them all, because Jesus is the Creator of even the most glorious beings, the angels. This is the way Hebrews asserts that Jesus is God like the Father is God and not like creatures.

The theme of Jesus as a new Moses is familiar to us from Matthew's Gospel. During the Sermon on the Mount, Jesus repeatedly references the **Torah**, which was understood to have been given to Moses directly. He then includes his own extra teaching on the topic which shows that the Torah is not only from God, but that he himself has the authority to modify it. So, for example, we saw Matt 5:27–28: "You have heard that it was said, 'You shall not commit adultery.' But I say to you, everyone who looks at a woman with lust has already committed adultery with her in his heart." In this case, Jesus demonstrates an authority superior to that of Moses. Hebrews takes a more direct line, but does so in continuity with this theme in Matthew. First, the author of Hebrews states that Jesus was faithful just as Moses was faithful.

He goes on to say that Jesus "is worthy of more 'glory' than Moses, as the founder of a house has more 'honor' than the house itself" (Heb 3:3). The author here is recognizing that the founder of the house of Israel, the house of the church, and indeed the house of all creation is none other than Jesus. Though Moses is important, Jesus is immeasurably more so.

Several chapters in Hebrews connect Jesus to the **Temple**, high priest, and the **covenant** which God made with the Jews. The focus on the Temple and the high priest represent the Jewish people's communion with God. This communion must be seen first and foremost as a gift from God. This gift is at the center of the story of God reaching out to the Jewish people in order to provide them with the order and structure of life lived in his presence. For this reason, God gave the Torah to govern and organize all major aspects of social life. Similarly, the Temple and the priestly servants of the Temple, especially the high priest, were given so that the Jewish people could offer their devotion and service to God in a uniquely religious way. The gifts of the Torah and the Temple demonstrate God's love for the Jews and indeed for all people.

The identification of Jesus as a new kind of high priest is central to Hebrews, functioning similarly to the way that Jesus is presented as above the angels and above Moses. At the beginning of chapter 7, Hebrews connects Jesus to the priest named Melchizedek, whom we saw briefly in Gen 14. Hebrews highlights how very little information Genesis gave to explain who this priest was, and it uses this lack of information as a springboard to draw out a connection with Jesus. It states, "Without father, mother, or ancestry, without beginning of days or end of life, thus made to resemble the Son of God, he remains a priest forever" (Heb 7:3). We already saw the importance of genealogical lists in both the Old Testament as well as in Matthew's Gospel. **Genealogies** give us critical information about the relationships God forms with families and peoples, and they show us that God cares for both individuals and groups. In the case of Hebrews, the author used the lack of information about Melchizedek as a way of symbolizing Jesus' eternal birth from the Father, as well as his possession of eternal qualities. Other aspects of Jesus as high priest will be addressed in a later section. Here, it is most important to understand that Jesus' superiority as high priest derives from his eternal identity as God and that Hebrews emphasizes God's love for Israel and all people as being found through a relationship with Jesus.

First John and the Antichrists

One significant element in John's first letter (1 John) is the way in which he challenges false teachers. He calls them "antichrists." First John 2:18 states, "Children, it is the last hour; and just as you heard that the antichrist was coming, so now many antichrists have appeared." "Antichrists" may seem like a shocking word to many readers. We are used to demonic and satanic images from popular culture's use of "antichrist," such as found in TV shows and movies. First John is making a connection to the ultimate evil spiritual power with the reference to "the antichrist," but his characterization of "antichrists" targets those giving a false version of Christian teaching. It is essentially the claim that perverting the truth about Jesus is far worse than images we might have about demons. John's Gospel likewise connected all things related to God to light and all things related to sin and evil to the darkness. The assertion in 1 John that all false teachers are antichrists is certainly quite strong, but it is a little less dramatic than an initial reading might suggest.

John warns against the real destruction which the false teachers cause, but it can be easy to miss what the false teaching really is about. In chapter 2, John puts it this way: "Who is the liar? Whoever denies that Jesus is the Christ. Whoever denies the Father and the Son, this is the antichrist" (1 John 2:22). As we know from the rest of the letter and John's Gospel, the **Christ** is the one who brings salvation to humanity. The Christ is Jesus, who is the eternal Word. He is the eternal Son of God. In the first and second centuries AD, it was possible to accept simple monotheism and thus belief in the Father. As we have seen again and again, Christianity proclaims that Jesus is the Christ. But for Christianity, the only true understanding of Jesus Christ must be based also on the ability to say that Jesus is God, like the Father is God. To confess that the one God is Father, Son, and Holy Spirit is the central and defining doctrine of Christianity. Therefore, those who deny that the Son is the Christ or that the Father and Son must be spoken of together as the one God (along with the Spirit) is denying the message of salvation which Christianity offers. If Jesus is not God the Son, his death and **resurrection** cannot be seen as bringing healing to all of humanity.

A second section in 1 John helps to clarify even more specifically what the false teachers thought. First John demands that the community "test the spirits" (1 John 4:1). By testing the spirits, John means that the community should make sure that all teachers are those who teach the genuine faith. John writes, "This is how you can know the Spirit of God: every spirit that acknowledges Jesus Christ come in the flesh belongs to God, and every spirit that does not acknowledge Jesus does not belong to God" (1 John 4:2–3). Here we are at the real crux of the false teaching. John knows that many only give lip service to the Father and Son. But even if one acknowledges that Jesus is the **Christ**, the denial that Jesus actually came in the flesh is, according to John, an important layer of the insidious and damaging ideas of these false teachers. Anything other than the Son taking on a human nature (i.e. "come in the flesh") means that our salvation would be thrown out. Salvation according to Christianity is the salvation of all our human parts, including both our souls and our bodies. The Gospel of John made the same points: "And the Word became flesh and made his dwelling among us" (John 1:14). This is why the Father sent the Son: "that the world might be saved through him" (John 3:17). Although not getting into further developments and details, this is exactly the train of thought 1 John has in mind: "Moreover, we have seen and testify that the Father sent his Son as savior of the world" (1 John 4:14). The various writers of the New Testament confirm that our salvation depends upon Jesus being simultaneously really divine and really human.

The false teachers to whom John refers are those who deny several fundamental teachings of the church. Such false teachers may use the names of "Father" and "Son." They may speak about Jesus as the Christ. But, they do not teach the faith of the church. We might ask: How could this be dangerous or something serious enough to describe as the work of "antichrists"? The danger is simple: false teaching leads to a missed or confused relationship with God. In a connected way, false teachings can lead people to reject the promise of salvation as God offers it. The church's teaching that the Son came in the flesh assures us that God loves us so much that he made sure we can have salvation through his own death and resurrection. Such a death and resurrection (and therefore such a teaching about salvation) is only possible if God the Son really did come in the flesh. 1 John thus argues that to use words "Father," "Son," and "Christ" and *not* be teaching about the **Trinity** and the **Incarnation** is to lead people away from the truth and away from the clearest and best relationship we can have with God.

The language of 1 John's condemnation of the heresy of those denying the Trinity and the Incarnation is strong. It is strong like the language of Hebrews when that letter sharply warns against rejecting Jesus as the fulfillment and climax of the Jewish tradition. In both cases, the danger of changing or ignoring what the Son did for the world when he became Jesus is equally bad for people. The rejection of Christianity once it has been received and believed (apostasy) as well as corrupted teachings within Christianity (heresy) sends people into a darkness of ignorance and confusion. Both texts are trying to show that life in the faith of the church is marked by true understanding and love. In the next section, that last topic—love—will be treated as the experience which is found through true teachings.

The Love which Redeems and Restores

Christianity teaches that human beings are in a state of separation from God which is caused entirely by our own sin. As already described, many believe that this teaching contradicts the goodness we find in ourselves, in others, and in the world in general. It does not. But it does directly challenge the incorrect teachings that we as human beings are in good shape and that we do not need a savior.

The Bible as a whole never flinches at human sin and corruption. This sounds like a very negative perspective about human beings and about human life. Hopefully, this study of the Bible has shown that an awareness of humanity's darkness is neither the beginning nor the end of the story. We have seen how God works to redeem human beings and bring them back into a relationship with him. The variety of scriptural selections this book covers repeatedly makes this clear. Though we were responsible for turning away from God and corrupting the nature God gave us, it is God who, time and again, acts for our salvation. We need God to teach us, to lead us, and ultimately to transform us as our Savior.

Looking back at Hebrews, we can reflect again on the initiative God takes to bring about human redemption. The author reminds his readers that it was God who made an oath to Abraham to bless and multiply his descendants (Heb 6:14). But the multiplication of people is not in and of itself the blessing. Rather, the most important blessing for any parent is to have children who live on and who eventually do not have to suffer from sin and death. For this reason, Hebrews points to Jesus as God the Son who became our high priest: "For we do not have a high priest who is unable to sympathize with our weaknesses, but one who has similarly been tested in every way, yet without sin" (Heb 4:15). Like the Jewish high priest who made sacrifices for the people to be forgiven and healed, Hebrews identifies Jesus as a high priest without sin. But Jesus is also the sacrifice for sin because he is perfect and pure. Hebrews states:

> But when Christ came as high priest of the good things
> that have come to be, passing through the greater and
> more perfect tabernacle not made by hands, that is, not
> belonging to this creation, he entered once for all into
> the sanctuary, not with the blood of goats and calves but
> with his own blood, thus obtaining eternal redemption.
> (Heb 9:11–12)

Hebrews shows that the Jerusalem **Temple**, the priests, and the sacrifices are **types** of the one true and final Temple, priest, and sacrifice. All three of these things are God himself. Jesus, who is

God the Son, is the true Temple. In that Temple, Jesus acts as both high priest and sacrifice. First John understands the very same logic of the Christian message. For this reason, 1 John can point to those who reject the Trinity and the Incarnation as those who are leading people away from salvation.

Hebrews focuses on what is lost when Christians turn away from a fullness of life through faith in Christ. One of those things is love for each other, leading the author to urge his readers: "Let mutual love continue" (Heb 13:1). Apostasy threatens the community's ability to live in mutual love through gratitude of God's redeeming sacrifice. First John, on the other hand, uses love as the central idea that expresses life within the church. First John emphasizes the danger of heresy which rejects the Trinity and the Incarnation. The most important factor which John sees as associated with such false teachings is the loss of love. In light of this, John gives a new commandment which essentially repeats ideas which Jesus teaches. First John clarifies what a life lived in Christian faith equates to: "Whoever says he is in the light, yet hates his brother, is still in the darkness. Whoever loves his brother remains in the light, and there is nothing in him to cause a fall" (1 John 2:9–10). True Christian faith must always equate to love.

Hebrews and 1 John both emphasize the centrality of God's love. In Hebrews, Jesus' Incarnation and sacrifice make salvation possible and hence the ability to continue with mutual love for each other. First John picks up on this idea and emphasizes God's love as the source of the Christian ability to love each other. John writes, "The way we came to know love was that he laid down his life for us; so we ought to lay down our lives for our brothers" (1 John 3:16). John really means that the human experience of love changes because of God's death and resurrection. He is not denying that human beings can experience love in general. But after knowing that God became a human being in order to die and rise for the salvation of his children, John is saying that the human experience of love can only be elevated in communion with God. The pinnacle of human love can only be found in the love which is returned to God who loves us to the point of dying for us. The Son's **Passion** is the only thing which can restore us to our relationship with God and, therefore, to truly loving relationships with each other.

Conclusion

Apostasy and heresy are both ideas which make little sense apart from God's love for us and our love for God and each other. Hebrews and 1 John are not condemning actions or teachings because the authors of these texts are disagreeable and want to impose their opinions on others. They condemn apostasy and heresy because they believe that real damage is done to people who turn away from the teachings and life of the church. Faith is not just accepting one system of belief over another. From the Christian perspective, the elements of faith which God reveals are the most important truths which human beings can know, and these truths allow us the most meaningful lives possible. Hebrews 11 gives testimony to the many generations of people who lived exemplary lives of faith, including Noah, Abraham, and Moses. From the Christian perspective, the faith of these ancient people now is amplified by the relationship God makes possible because of the Incarnation. To deny the Trinity, the Incarnation, or the Christian faith in general is seen by both texts as departing from a relationship with God which fuels the highest form of human life possible. This life, which is life lived within the faith of the church, is characterized by the highest form of love possible for human beings. Such a love can only originate within God, and God alone can fuel the purest form of love which human beings have for God and others.

Study and Reflection Questions

1. How does the Great Commission given by Jesus to the church (Matt 28) relate to ideas of protecting the church's faith as found in Hebrews and 1 John?

2. How does God's love shape the insistence in both Hebrews and 1 John that we must remain on the path of faith as defined by the church's teachings?

3. What is a detail or verse in each of the texts which you think connects to something you read in the Gospels?

Conclusion

Here at the end of our study, we can take a moment to reflect on where we have been and what we have seen. Our work began by considering God's singular work in creating everything and everyone. We saw the way the first sin led to humanity's descent into chaos and depravity. But then we witnessed God beginning a new period in his interactions with humanity through the very specific actions with Abraham, Sarah, and their descendants. God made a special **covenant** with these people, the Jews, in order to prepare the rest of the world to see his work come to fulfillment through that "light to the nations." We also saw through the book of Jonah that God's covenant and relationship with the Jews never meant that he ignored the rest of the world. The climax of God's preparation to draw all people towards himself came with his own presence as Jesus among his **chosen people**. Finally, we saw how the Holy Spirit empowered the church to continue God's work in the world, which he himself began and continues to empower. This is the basis of the Christian worldview, and it has proven gloriously attractive to billions of people over the past 2,000 years.

Despite the many hundreds of years it took to write and the complicated process of its editing and collecting, the Bible tells a consistent story about human history and life. All of human history begins, continues, and will end in God's presence. This does not mean that God controls us. God gave us free will so that we can respond in love to the love he gives us. We are free to abuse our free wills. We are free to make ourselves slaves to everything and anything less than God. Or we can use our free wills to humbly accept God's loving gift of life. Both of these ideas are found in the stories and teachings of the Bible. Even more importantly, a consistent element found throughout the whole Bible is that God does not wait for us to decide on our own. God has always spoken and acted to give us fullness of life. God has never really been silent, nor has God ever stopped being present to the world.

Particular studies of the Bible can help us see and appreciate incredibly important biblical themes. Even major themes can be hard to see sometimes because of the Bible being made up of so many texts. Limiting the number of texts used in a study such as this and trying to keep a focus on a smaller set of topics, however, can more easily highlight the grandeur of God's communications with us. Other studies like this book could focus on God's mercy, on covenant, on faith, or on justice. These are just a few of the themes which one could look at through a selection of biblical texts. This book, however, has been about *God's loving communication*. Many people today see no good evidence that God acts in history and in us. Many also do not see evidence for claiming that God acts out of love in order to bring us into loving relationships. The Bible and the Christian faith address the fear that God is not loving, and they allow us to see the world from the perspective of God's love. This perspective begins with the acknowledgement that God always speaks, acts, and invites us into communion with him.

Glossary

Chosen people: The Jewish people as understood to have been selected by God to receive special blessings. These blessings include the promises made to Abraham of becoming a great nation and possessing the promised land. These blessings also include living in communion with God through the Torah and, for a time, with the Temple in Jerusalem.

Christ: The Greek word meaning "anointed one." It is the Greek version of the Hebrew word "Messiah." Both "Messiah" and "Christ" are the title for the person the Jewish prophets spoke of who would be sent by God to bring peace and salvation to the Jewish people. See also, **Messiah**.

Covenant: Meaning a pledge, alliance, or contract, its biblical usage usually refers to the special relationship God forms with the Jews as his chosen people. It contains a deep sense of God's insistence that he established a relationship which will endure. This special relationship is understood by Christianity to be found for all people through the church.

Exodus: The event in which God sent Moses to lead the chosen people out of slavery and oppression in Egypt to eventual liberation in the promised land.

Genealogy: A generational list documenting the origins of a person or family.

General revelation: God's revelations to humanity through means of having made us with rationality and free will. This form of revelation allows human beings to know some truths about God through creation and our nature without needing God to communicate further to the world in a special way. This term is synonymous with the theological term "natural revelation."

Gentile: Everyone who is not a Jew by birth or practice.

Incarnation: God the Son's joining himself to human nature by being conceived through Mary. This includes the Christian teaching that Jesus is both fully divine and fully human, because he is God the Son.

Messiah: The Hebrew word meaning "anointed one." This is the title of the anticipated person spoken of by the Jewish prophets who would be sent by God to bring peace and salvation to the Jewish people. See also, **Christ**.

Passion: The term referring to Jesus' trial, suffering, and death.

Resurrection: The term referring to Jesus' rising from the dead in both his body and soul, after his Passion.

Salvation history: God's progressive actions through history to bring salvation to humanity.

Shema: A central Jewish declaration of faith found in Deut 6:4–9.

Special revelation: God actively coming into contact with his creation in order to offer grace, love, and direction to human beings. This is synonymous with the theological term "historical revelation."

Temple (in Jerusalem): The Temple built by Solomon in Jerusalem as the special place of Jewish worship and sacrifice. God's unique presence there allowed it to serve as a place by and through which the Jewish people could celebrate God, acknowledge their sins, and gain forgiveness.

Ten Commandments: The commandments which God wrote for Moses on stone tablets and which are given in Exod 20:1–17. They summarize basic duties owed to God and to human beings.

Tetragrammaton: This word means "four letters," and corresponds to the name "YHWH." It is God's personal name which he tells to Moses from the Burning Bush. Usually, the name is given in English as "**Yahweh**."

Torah: Translated as "Law" or "Instruction," the Torah gives a comprehensive guide to living for the Jews and is found in the Old Testament. It is intended to support the loving relationship between the people with God and with each other.

Trinity: The term referring to the reality that the One God, or the one divine nature, can only be understood as the distinct Persons of the Father, Son, and Holy Spirit, who, because they share the one divine nature, are each fully God.

Type/Typology: Terms descriptive of one event or person in the Scriptures as foreshadowing or being a kind of model of something or someone later in the text. Christians mostly see in the Old Testament such elements pointing to Jesus himself.

Yahweh: God's personal name which he reveals to Moses from the burning bush. See also, **Tetragrammaton**.